A Call For Hawaiian Sovereignty

Michael Kioni Dudley

Keoni Kealoha Agard

with an Introduction by
John Dominis Holt

Nā Kāne O Ka Malo Press
Honolulu, Hawai'i
1993

Cover artwork: Lalepa Ah Sam
Cover design: Belknap Imaging, Honolulu

Published by Na Kane O Ka Malo Press
Copyright 1990 by Michael Kioni Dudley
Printed in the United States of America

Inquiries should be addressed to:

> Na Kane O Ka Malo Press
> P.O. Box 970
> Waipahu, Hawai'i 96797-0970
> Telephone: (808) 672-8888

The paper used in this publication meets the minimum requirements of American Nation Standard for Information Sciences -- Permanence of Paper for Printed Library Materials, ANSI 239.48-1984.

Previously published as *A Hawaiian Nation II   A Call for Hawaiian Sovereignty,* ISBN 1-878751-03-4 in 1990.
Second Printing   1990
Centennial Commemoration Edition 1993
This fourth printing   1997

Library of Congress Catalog Card Number: 90-184941

ISBN: 1-878751-09-3

Dedicated to

The Native Hawaiian People

Contents

Introduction

Hawaiians of old were as close to the land as any people can be. People in the entire population were in daily touch with the land and the sea. If they did not fish the seas or tend the fishponds, or work in the *taro lo'i*, the fields of sweet potato, or the groves of breadfruit, they saw others doing those things all around them.

Life was essentially routine, fairly simple, but rich in poetry, symbol, myth and art. Hawaiians were creators of beautiful objects: sculptures, ornately carved tools and utensils, feather capes, helmets, *kahilis* and *leis*, and other objects of adornment. They took the celebration of life, people, and nature to inspiring heights in chants and the *hula*.

Captain Cook, the first white man to reach the islands, observed in 1778, that Hawaiians were a lively, productive, friendly people who in his opinion had brought the cultural conglomerate of Pacific peoples to the highest point of development. Captain Vancouver, arriving ten years later, wrote in his journals that the native Hawaiian as farmer and horticulturist was second to none.

The Hawaiian's successful relationship with nature was the outgrowth of his world view—that man participates in a consciously interrelating cosmic community in which all of the beings of nature protect and care for one another. *A Hawaiian Nation I Man, Gods and Nature*, deals extensively with the traditional Hawaiian view. Published as a companion volume to this book, it would well be read by those seeking a greater understanding of Hawaiian culture.

The arrival of Cook changed life in the islands. The magical world of song, dance, hard work, hard sex, and sensible social organization was replaced by foreign ways and foreign values, and eventually by foreign overthrow of our kingdom and foreign control of our lands and lives.

Kioni Dudley and Keoni Agard have traced the ignominious history of plunder and overthrow in this volume. *A Call for Hawaiian Sovereignty* is a powerful book. Dudley and Agard don't shrink from their responsibility to set the record straight. Their history of the dispossession of the Hawaiian people hits all the main points and tells it like it is—in a highly documented yet extremely readable, fascinating way. Many of the details have been brought tog ether in one place for the first time in this volume. Step by step, Dudley and Agard detail what really happened in the rape of the Hawaiian nation. The facts they present weigh hard against Americans and America, and call for restitution.

The book also presents a short history of the sovereignty movement, detailing the growing frustration and the increasingly frequent protests which have taken place over the last two decades, as well as the organization that has gone on in preparation for reclaiming sovereign-nation status.

Dudley and Agard also give a good account of where the sovereignty movement is today. And they present a number of brief but very clearly explained "models for nationhood" which have been proposed by various sovereignty groups.

These books will do much to educate our people—and those who are interested in our people—about our past, and about what we can make of our future.

Return of lands and recognition of sovereignty has been a long time coming. When I was a child, Hawaiians were ashamed of being Hawaiian. One of my great aunts and her friends used to eat Hawaiian food in very private circumstances. They also made it a point to never speak Hawaiian in public, only amongst themselves. To be Hawaiian was *déclassé*.

We never dreamed of having our own land again, of being a sovereign nation. But that day is now near.

Deep in the soul of all Hawaiians is a desire to speak our own language, to relate with the natural world publicly and unashamedly as our ancestors did, to think our own thoughts, to pursue our own aspirations, to develop our own arts, to worship our own gods, to follow our own moral system, to see our own people when we look around us, to be Hawaiian again. We long to make contributions to the world as Hawaiians, to exist as a Hawaiian nation, to add "a Hawaiian presence" to the world community. Establishment of a sovereign Hawaiian nation will give us that chance.

Imua! Puka i ka Lanakila.

John Dominis Holt

Preface

"Nationhood for the Native Hawaiians!" Such a thought would have been unthinkable ten years ago. Yet today the sovereignty movement is strong. A number of pro-nation groups are meeting regularly, planning, working out details, and educating other Hawaiians. One pro-sovereignty group has held constitutional conventions in which delegates elected statewide have drafted, and later revised, a constitution. Churches both locally and on the national level have taken positions of support for Hawaiian sovereignty. The Hawai'i State Legislature has voted a resolution of support. Congress has apologized to the Hawaiian people for America's illegal actions in the overthrow of the Hawaiian nation. And there are bills before the Congress for restoration of the Hawaiian nation.

While many Americans, perhaps, are not aware of it, there are numerous precedents for native American sovereign nations within America. There are 309 distinct nations existing by treaty within the territorial limits of the United States. American Indians, Aleuts, and Inuits comprise the first 308. The 309th is the United States of America. Native American nations enjoy some areas of complete sovereignty and some areas of limited sovereignty. They have their own territory, their own governmental structures, their own laws; they collect their own taxes; and they are protected by American federal law in the practice of their culture and religion.

But why would native Hawaiians want their own nation? Hawai'i fought hard for statehood. Can it be that the same people who were so anxious for union with the United States now want independence?

For the most part, No, it is not those who most wanted statehood who now seek sovereignty. Those seeking sovereignty are native Hawaiians, Polynesian people whose ancestors, after navigating over thousands of miles of open ocean on great voyaging expeditions of exploration, discovered and settled the islands at about the time of Christ. Hawaiians seeking sovereignty are descendants of the Hawaiian people whom Captain Cook found living in the islands when he arrived in 1778, descendants of the people whom the missionaries arrived to Christianize in 1820.

Hawaiians seeking nationhood are the native people to whom the white man introduced money, whose king the white man coerced into dividing up the islands and instituting private land ownership, and who lost their lands when the white man then used his money to buy up the private property.

The people seeking sovereignty are native Hawaiians who watched as diseases of the white man reduced their numbers from around a million in 1778 to less than forty thousand a century later: more than nine hundred thousand of their race suffering and dying of the sicknesses brought by people who came to "civilize" them.

Hawaiians seeking sovereignty are the native people whose government was overthrown in 1893 by a group comprised primarily of American citizens and others with dual American-Hawaiian citizenship, in a coup at least partly planned by the American Minister to Hawai'i and supported by troops he called into the city from an American battleship.

Hawaiians seeking restoration of their nation are those native people living in the islands who, in the years after Annexation as a Territory of the United States, saw laws passed forbidding them to practice aspects of their culture or to speak their own language.

No, Hawaiians who are seeking sovereignty and the return of their lands are not the same people who were so anxious for admission into the Union a generation ago. Those seeking statehood then have mostly profited from it. Native Hawaiians seeking sovereignty generally have not. They look around them today and see many of their Hawaiian brothers and sisters and children without food, without shelter, without skills, education, and jobs...in this "land of plenty." Those seeking nationhood are native Hawaiian people "dispossessed" in their own homeland.

A Call for Hawaiian Sovereignty tells the history of their dispossession. It tells about the rise of their sovereignty movement, and discusses the models for nationhood which various pro-sovereignty groups are proposing.

This book, however, is not intended to represent a complete picture of the subject of native Hawaiian sovereignty. It is merely an introduction, an overview in outline, of what native Hawaiian sovereignty is all about. It is written as an instructive tool to inform the general public on this important issue. It can be useful to clarify how far the movement has come and what has been done. Providing a basic outline of "models for sovereignty" which have been proposed is important at this time. This area needs much work: so much more research, brainstorming, community discussion, and debate are required before the Hawaiian community can formulate clearly what choices are available, let alone which model of nationhood is most appropriate.

There is a need for groups to take up specific, clearly defined models of nationhood, to live with them and work with them, and to flush out the values and deficiencies of their models through public presentations and debates. Various sovereignty groups have already identified with some of the models. But a number of interesting variations have no proponents "wearing them and getting their feel," and exploring their strengths and weaknesses.

It is also perhaps time for the Hawaiian community to begin viewing the various sovereignty groups as political parties and the nationhood models they propound as their platforms--the place of the political party being to vie for the public's votes through presenting their models and trying to win popular support. Such a process would at the same time give the community a chance to observe those presenting views, judging them as candidates for future office in the government of the Hawaiian nation.

These are exciting times for the Hawaiian community and for the non-Hawaiian citizens of the state. To be a part of the birth or rebirth of a nation is a privilege given so few humans. As happened in the establishment of the American nation, some decisions will be monumental, affecting generations for hundreds of years to come. No one can tell which decisions these will be. We must make decisions now, while the attention and enthusiasm are with us. Yet under this pressure, we must be so careful to provide the best circumstances possible for our posterity. Basic to wise decision making is being well informed about what really happened in the past, and also where we really are today. This book aspires to provide that background.

Acknowledgments

There are many people who in various ways have influenced this book--many who have helped in the production, many who have been longer range supports for the authors.

Among the people who deserve our *mahalo ā nui loa* for the book production are:

Lalepa Ah Sam who did the powerful artwork on the cover. Lalepa was Professor Dudley's student at the University of Hawai'i in 1981-1983. His bold and striking art contribution attests to his love for his people and to his interest and support for the sovereignty movement.

Henry Bennett, of Independent Resources, has been very helpful both with editorial assistance and in guiding the book through publication.

Buzz Belknap and his staff at Belknap Imaging were such a pleasure to work with in creating the cover design.

Professor Stephen Boggs, Ph.D., for many years deeply involved in the Hawaiian scene, has been very generous with his time, reading early versions of the text and making suggestions.

Kioni Dudley expresses his gratitude:

I want to salute the young men of the Nānākuli Hawaiian boys' club, *Nā Alaka'i Mua* (The Leaders of Tomorrow). Their enthusiasm for their Hawaiianness and their willingness to **work** on projects to preserve their cultural heritage has been a continuing inspiration to me. Much of the drive I have had to finish this book has been powered by the desire to help bring about a Hawaiian nation for them.

Many people of Nānākuli have worked with me in efforts to get the public school system to educate Hawaiian children as Hawaiians. Deeply involving themselves in activities this book so roundly supports, they too have been a continuing source of encouragement.

I also want to pay tribute to my parents, Willard and Melva Dudley, for the high priority they placed on education for their children, and for their unfailing belief in my visions and dreams during the years of pursuing my doctoral degree and working on these books.

I want to recognize my aunt, Marie Mac Donald, for her enthusiastic support over the years. I am grateful too to my mother-in-law, Yoshiko Kamioka, for her generous encouragement of this project.

Daniel Kenji San Miguel, my stepson, did the drawings found in this book's companion volume, *Man, Gods, and Nature.* Patiently working with me through the many revisions required to give form to what I could not visualize and could describe only vaguely, his original drawings have captured my intent and expressed it with fascinating creativity.

Daniel's brother, Luis Kazuo San Miguel, was a great help to me in the early, most difficult stages of breaking through to an understanding of the Hawaiian world view. *A Hawaiian Nation I Man, Gods, and Nature* is dedicated to Luis.

The person who stands out as having given the most in support of all my endeavors is my wife Doris (Kolika)

Sadako Dudley. I am grateful for her love and for the many sacrifices she has made over the twelve years of study, research, and writing that I have contributed to these books. My greatest treasure, my best friend, and my most willing helper, the books would never have been completed without her.

Keoni Agard expresses his gratitude:

As early as 1973, two individuals in my life were inviting and encouraging me to attend various Hawaiian community meetings. They were my father, John M. Agard, and my uncle, Louis K. Agard. We attended many meetings of the Council of Hawaiian Organizations which was comprised of some twelve to thirteen individual Hawaiian groups. I sat, observed, and learned about the vital issues confronting the Hawaiian nation, my interest and participation spurred on by the presence and intense involvement of my father and my uncle. Had I not been introduced by them to topics such as reparations to Native Hawaiians and Hawaiian sovereignty, my life course would have taken a different path.

Along with my father and uncle, I want to thank my mother, Joanna K. Agard, for standing solidly behind me in my work commitment to the Native Hawaiian community over the years.

I thank the entire administration and staff of Alu Like, Inc. (a non-profit organization geared toward achieving social and economic self sufficiency for Native Hawaiians), for the opportunity I had to serve on their statewide board of directors between 1979-1984. That experience enriched my understanding and commitment to serve the Native Hawaiian community.

I thank the Native Hawaiian Legal Corporation's attorneys and staff for their efforts in conducting sovereignty conferences to educate the community.

I thank all my Native Hawaiian clients who have believed in me and believed in their right to stand up in the face of imposing odds and fight to rectify past injustices.

I thank my parents in law, James and Dora Akamine, for their devoted support and encouragement.

I thank my wife, Lynette Lei Akamine Agard, for her loving support, patience, understanding and valuable input during the course of this long endeavor.

Michael Kioni Dudley

Keoni Kealoha Agard

Honolulu, Hawai'i

A History of
Dispossession

WHEN THE WHITE MAN FIRST APPEARED in Hawai'i, there were about a million Hawaiians living in the islands, at best counts.[1] The lands were lush and verdant, the seas filled with fish. Life was good. The people were healthy, vigorous, and happy.

Hawaiians were people of the land. Chiefs frequently worked the land along with commoners. Kamehameha I, for instance, loved the hard work of raising *kalo* (taro), and could often be found in his *kalo lo'i* through the entire working day—from dawn until the heat of the day and then again from later afternoon until dark.

From ancient days the *ali'i nui*—the ruling high chief or king—had charge of the lands. It would be incorrect to say the lands belonged to him but, supported by his special nurturing role in relation to surrounding nature, he controlled the lands and had total say over them. The chiefs under him who held land did so at his pleasure, and their lands returned to the *ali'i nui* at their deaths. Private ownership of land was unknown.

Since islands are roughly circular, the traditional land divisions in Hawai'i resemble the slices of a pie. The *ahupua'a*, the subdivisions of a district, can be pictured as thin slices of the pie. The narrow end of the *ahupua'a* is at a central or inland mountain top, and it broadens out as it progresses towards the shore and out into the sea. Each

1

ahupua'a was for the most part self-sufficient, producing everything needed by the people living within its boundaries. People did not live in villages: their homes were scattered over the area of the *ahupua'a*. Hawaiians had no money and did not barter. But those who fished in the sea needed to fill out their diet with the crops that others raised in the uplands, and the uplanders needed fish. Society was based on generosity and communal concern. Fishermen gave freely, and farmers gave freely. And all flourished. A *konohiki,* or overseer, assured that a constant flow of products moved through the *ahupua'a,* meeting everybody's needs.

When Captain Cook arrived in the islands, the Hawaiians, whose gods were thought to appear in human form, mistook him for a god. Fascinating stories have come down telling how Hawaiians thought the clothes Cook wore were different-colored layers of his skin, how the shiny buttons on his coat were thought to be flashing lights from within him, and how, because of his pipe, the "god" was thought to exude smoke, just as did the goddess of the volcano, Pele. Cook was only in the islands for a few days in 1778 before a storm forced him away. When he returned a year later, word of his arrival had spread through all the islands, even those hundreds of miles distant. The venereal disease brought by his men had also spread just as broadly, and with the disease its accompanying suffering, insanity, and death.[2] The destruction of the Hawaiian race had begun.

Like all human beings, the Hawaiians had only their own experience to rely on when approaching and judging what they encountered. When the Western world came to Hawai'i, the Westerners had knowledge of life, culture, and refinements on various continents. The explorers and traders were sharp businessmen who knew value and knew worthlessness. By contrast, the simple island experience of the Hawaiians was so limited! They did not sell Manhattan island for a box of shiny beads. Not knowing what to prize, they lost far more.

Traders introduced bartering and introduced money. And the Hawaiian chiefs made tragic mistakes in learning their use. The sandalwood trade is one example. Within one generation Hawai'i was almost completely stripped of its sandalwood forests and, for the most part, all that the Hawaiians had to show for their loss were great debts to the traders. Worse, great numbers of people were brought off the lands and away from their traditional occupations and lifestyles to work the sandalwood trade—the first serious tear in the fabric of traditional society and in the flow of food and services in the *ahupua'a*.

Hawaiian chiefs imitated the Westerners. They had so many "different" things, and the new, "different" things were thought of as better. Traditional ways came to be viewed as "not as good as Western ways." And what lay in the way of "becoming Western" had to go. Kamehameha I held on during his lifetime, but at his death in 1819 the powerful chiefess Ka'ahumanu effected the laying aside of traditional societal laws (the *kapu* system) and the religion that supported it.

Unintentionally, this act laid open the way for the work of the first missionaries. They arrived within the year, bringing with them two convictions: that theirs was the one true religion, and that their society was superior to that of the Hawaiians. Both convictions they taught with equal vigor. Hawaiians who attended missionary schools tried to assimilate Western knowledge into their own Hawaiian thought framework, while continuing to function from a Hawaiian perspective and from within Hawaiian culture. The missionaries own children, however, understood their lessons from the Western, economic, life-view of their parents, and from the Protestant work ethic—that "God rewards the virtuous, hard-working man with wealth." As they matured, the focus of the missionaries' children was entirely Western, like that of their parents. No one seriously considered viewing life from the Hawaiian perspective, or contemplated what life could be like if they maintained and promoted "the Hawaiian way." Instead, they set themselves to becoming virtuously wealthy **Westerners** in the Hawaiians' lands.

Traditionally the *ali'i nui* controlled land tenure in Hawai'i. When white people came to the islands, they were occasionally awarded land to live on. But the traditional meaning of "give you lands" included the perhaps unexpressed proviso, "which you will hold at my pleasure." The whole episode in which Kamehameha III was forced to temporarily cede control of his country to Britain in 1843 came about because of a misunderstanding the British consul had with the king over private land ownership. The consul claimed permanent ownership over lands sold to him by lesser chiefs, but those chiefs had only held them at the king's pleasure.

While private ownership was a foreign concept to Hawaiians, it was a necessary part, indeed the basis, of Western economic activity.

Almost from the time of their arrival, the missionaries exerted some influence over the kings. As relations with the outside world became more complex in the late 1830s and '40s, King Kamehameha III began to look for people to assist the kingdom who were educated in the Western ways. He found a number of missionaries willing to take positions in government. Other capable white newcomers also joined, taking some of the government's most powerful positions. By the end of 1844 there were fourteen white men in government service. All three of the most important members of the king's cabinet were white.[3]

To a man, the whites in government were convinced that the capitalistic economic system was necessary and good for Hawai'i. They had known nothing else. They argued that if a man had a piece of property that he could call his own, he would work hard to make something of himself.[4] Private ownership would transform the Hawaiian society into a hardworking, industrious, and prosperous nation. The whites seemed incapable of realizing that Hawaiians in general could not think in a capitalistic way. One had to rely on his world of experience to provide the background for one's thoughts and actions. The Hawaiians had experienced only the *ahupua'a* life. Generosity and free giving were the very basis of the economic system at work in the ahupua'a: one **gave away** all his surplus. That way everybody was provided for. Capitalism demanded that one keep his surplus, that he deny it to others. Hawaiians could not understand why anyone would want to do that. Wealth was the accumulation of things of value which others wanted, and this made no sense to the Hawaiians. They could not handle the Westerner's system. The *ahupua'a* system, however, was familiar to them. They understood it. And it had been very efficient in providing for people's needs and in giving them direction. Instead of a new economic system which was foreign to them, what the Hawaiians desperately needed in the 1840s was for the government to reestablish and fortify the *ahupua'a* system.[5]

The famed Hawaiian intellectual and author David Malo and others saw this. In 1845 they collected thousands of names of native Hawaiians on Maui and on the island of Hawai'i petitioning the king to get rid of the white men (*haoles*) in government and to take a stand against private ownership. Repeated communications from these groups told the king that his white government officials would eventually take over the government and take the country away from the Hawaiians. These groups also told the king that if he allowed private ownership, the white man would use his great wealth to buy up all the land. Letters pointed out that current laws required that commoners be paid "in kind" rather than in cash. When land would be available, the whites would have money to buy the lands, but the commoners would not.[6] They pleaded, "Give us ten years to prepare our people to purchase the lands, so that when they are made available, they will stay in native hands."

Their cries fell on unheeding ears. The *haoles* (white men) would be kept in their powerful government positions "because they were needed," as the king said. The *haole* traders and merchants with whom the government had to deal were cunning, and the king and chiefs did not know enough of their ways and their laws to come out on top. White men in government had sworn their loyalty to the king, and they were needed now. But they would only fill positions for the interim—until Hawaiians were educated enough to take their places.[7]

It must be noted that some of these advisors were truly dedicated to the king and in every move tried to do what was best for the kingdom. They were just misguided. They hoped to get Hawaiian natives out of urban slums and back onto the land by creating a class of landed commoners who would work small, personally owned farms. Yet, through their miscalculation of the Hawaiians' ability to deal with private ownership, these advisors indeed were the direct cause of the Hawaiians losing their lands to the white foreigner.

As the 1840s progressed, Kamehameha III succumbed increasingly to the advice of the whites in his Cabinet. By the latter part of the decade, *haole* advisors had in fact completely taken over government decision making.[8] Then, using the experience of the temporary British takeover in 1843 as an example of something that could easily happen again, they scared an unwilling king and his chiefs into establishing private property.[9]

The *Mahele*

In 1848 Hawaiian lands were divided up. This "division" of lands is called the *mahele*. Originally the idea was to divide the land three ways: one-third each for the king, the chiefs, and the commoners.[10] As it turned out, the chiefs were given about one and a half million acres. Some land was also set aside for the Fort. The king kept about a million acres—the "crown lands" as they were later called. Most of the rest, roughly another one and a half million acres, was set aside as "government lands."[11]

According to the original plan, in 1850, two years after the land division took place, native Hawaiian commoners who had lived on a piece of property for the previous ten years would be allowed to make a claim to between one and two acres of land surrounding their homes. These were called *kuleana* claims. Since these claims would take place two years after the original division, the *kuleana* lands claimed would be portions taken from the chiefs' lands, the crown lands, or the government lands.

Additionally, portions of the "government lands" were also set aside for sale to native commoners who did not qualify for *kuleana* land claims.[12] *Kuleana* holders who wished to increase the size of their lands would also be able to do so by purchasing additional, inexpensive property from among the "government lands."[13]

Kamehameha III, who was initially strongly opposed to the idea of the *mahele*, was brought around to accepting it because of his concern for the number of native Hawaiian commoners who had come off the *ahupua'a* and were living destitute in the towns.[14] He came to believe that making the government lands available to them would encourage many of the jobless Hawaiians in the towns to return to the land.[15]

The "crown lands" and the "government lands" have become very important to the Hawaiian people today. Native Hawaiians claim that both belong exclusively to them and to no one else, and they want them returned to form part of the land base for the Hawaiian nation.

In regard to "government lands," part of the present claim centers around the questions of precisely whom the "government lands" were set aside to benefit, and who—according to the intent of the *mahele* itself—was allowed to buy them. Because these questions are so important, let us investigate them. First, who could purchase the land.

One purpose of the "government lands" was to provide income to run the government. Money would come from selling or leasing the lands. But from the beginning of *mahele* discussion among the chiefs, there had been clear statements that land would not go to non-Hawaiians. "A law enacted in August, 1843, had contained the statement: 'And it is hereby unanimously declared that we will neither give away or sell any lands in the future to foreigners, nor shall such gift or sale by any native be valid.'"[16] Similar later declarations reconfirmed this throughout the years of planning the *mahele*.[17]

In the preface to the list of "The Government Lands" in the *Book of the Mahele*, it is stated that the lands were set aside by the King and placed under the supervision of the Minister of the Interior and his successors, who, "at some time and for some reason, when it is thought best for the Government, might sell them **to native Hawaiian people**."[18] They were to be sold to native Hawaiian commoners for fifty cents an acre.[19]

Non-Hawaiians were not considered as possible purchasers. In 1847, a year before the final division in the *mahele*, small portions of land were **awarded** (not sold) to non-Hawaiian individuals, both in and out of the government, who either had previously held them "at the pleasure of the king" or who merited some reward at that time.[20] Those were the only non-Hawaiians who had, or were expected to have, any serious claim to land in the islands.

The "government lands," then, were set aside for purchase by native Hawaiian people alone.

Those purchases were to provide income for the government. Certainly, non-Hawaiian citizens would also profit from the running of the government. Can it be argued, then, that the "government lands" were set aside only to benefit Hawaiians, and not non-Hawaiians also?

In the first place, there were very few non-Hawaiians in the islands at the time of the *mahele* in 1848, probably between thirteen hundred and fifteen hundred. Native Hawaiians outnumbered non-Hawaiians almost one hundred to one.[21] Their small numbers alone kept non-Hawaiians from being a significant concern of the government.

Beyond that, very few non-Hawaiians were naturalized citizens of the Kingdom. Foreigners had been allowed to become naturalized Hawaiian citizens through taking an Oath of Allegiance to the Kingdom since 1838.[22] But until 1846 the Oath of Allegiance had included renunciation of allegiance to one's native country. Very few foreigners had been willing to take the drastic step of relinquishing their rights in a major country in order to become citizens in a small and very distant Polynesian kingdom.[23] Renunciation of former citizenship was dropped from the Oath in 1846. Less than two years then passed before the setting aside of the "government lands" at the final signing of the *Buke Mahele* (Book of the Mahele) in 1848.[24] Presumably the number of foreigners in the islands who became naturalized citizens had not increased radically in that two years.

By comparison with the roughly 100,000 native Hawaiian citizens in 1848, the fifteen hundred or so resident non-Hawaiians were a tiny minority. And the number of that tiny minority who had become naturalized citizens was so insignificant that they possibly never entered into Kamehameha III's consideration as also "to be benefitted by the government lands."

Further, since most non-Hawaiians had become naturalized citizens in order to marry native Hawaiians, they were Hawaiian family members anyway.[25] Their descendants would all have Hawaiian blood. There was thus little reason to think of them as "separate" and "individuated" non-Hawaiian beneficiaries of the government.

Additionally, there is strong reason to believe that Kamehameha III purposely avoided any reference to non-Hawaiians when he stated whom he intended to benefit from all aspects of the *mahele*. Throughout this period, native Hawaiians on the neighbor islands were petitioning and demonstrating against both the *haole*s in government and the possibility of Hawaiian land being sold to non-Hawaiians. The king himself had to go to Maui in 1845 to calm their fears.[26] But the calm had not lasted long. In 1848, the year of the *mahele* itself, "the natives of Maui, among whom were some careful students of foreign affairs, began to talk about storming the fort at Lahaina, and killing all the white men. Rumors at Honolulu put David Malo in the middle of the uproar again: he was supposed to have more than a thousand men in arms, ready to descend on Oahu."[27] In response to the protestors, Kamehameha III constantly reiterated that the *haole* presence in government was only transitory, and that they would remain only until Hawaiians could be trained to run the government. He was clearly committed to the idea that Hawai'i would be a Hawaiian nation—owned by Hawaiians and run by Hawaiians for the benefit of Hawaiians.

There is every reason to believe, then, that the King's specific intent was to include only native Hawaiians among those who would have lands and benefit from the government.

He thus began the *Buke Mahele* with the following:

> "Know you people by this document, that I am
> Kamehameha III, the King of this Hawaiian Archipelago
> by the grace of God. I hereby give completely and
> forever—and separate out for the chiefs and the people of
> my Kingdom—the lands written in this book,
> relinquishing all my rights and interest and wealth in
> them, **in order that my Chiefs and my Hawaiian people
> may dwell and establish themselves firmly upon the
> lands forever.**[28]

A quote from John Papa I'i, one of the Land Commissioners, confirms how the *mahele* was commonly understood.

> [Kamehameha III] divided the lands in the Great Mahele
> of 1848, believing the division would be permanent.
> [Because of this,] it was said that he was the greatest of
> kings, a royal parent who loved his Hawaiian people
> more than any other chief before him.[29]

By placing Kamehameha III and his actions in the *mahele* into the context of a long line of chiefs who ruled over only native Hawaiian people, it is clear that when I'i refers to "his Hawaiian people" whom this "royal parent" loved and permanently divided his lands among, he is speaking only of native Hawaiians. Non-Hawaiians were simply not included in the consideration, at least in the mind of John Papa I'i. And the evidence suggests that no one else at the time looked at the situation any differently.

When native Hawaiians, then, argue that at the time that the *mahele* was signed into law, the "government lands" were set aside for them and them alone, the evidence supports their claim. They alone could buy the land. They alone were the intended benefactors of the *mahele*. "Government lands"—and the rest of the islands—were set aside so that native Hawaiians might dwell upon them and establish themselves forever.

Despite the good intentions of the king, the *mahele* was one of the greatest disasters ever suffered by the Hawaiian people. It effectively handed over to white people, citizens and foreigners alike, ownership and control of the land. Kamehameha III was not the intellectual, strong willed, charismatic leader the times demanded. Shortly after signing the *mahele* in 1848, he began to drink heavily again. From May of 1849, he began to neglect his Privy Council meetings. As Lilikalā Kame'eleihiwa notes, between May 2, 1849, and September 30, 1850, the king missed thirty-six Privy Council meetings. Prior to this he had never missed any at all.[30] All of the modern changes, all of the pressures were too much for the king. He simply gave up. The dominant, white members of the Privy Council then ran the government.

In 1850 the commoners were to be allowed to claim *kuleana* lands and to purchase "government lands." But almost a month before the lands were opened to them, the Legislature confirmed the decision of the *haole*-dominated Privy Council allowing all residents, even foreigners, unrestricted rights to buy and sell lands.[31] Under *haole* supervision, the "government lands," so carefully set aside "forever" for his commoners by a loving king, were competed for: cash-poor commoners unaware of the meaning of land-title vs. shrewd *haoles*, some backed with almost unlimited wealth—just as Malo and the other petitioners had predicted.

The commoners hardly even entered the contest. Their life experiences had taught them to work the land under the direction of someone who would make sure they were provided for. Under the new system, they might have their own land to farm, but how would they get their crops to a market? And once there, how would they know how to bargain for a price? The *mahele* was doomed to failure because there was no marketing structure outside of the port towns to support private enterprise. The whole concept was too foreign and too complicated for the commoner. Uneducated, unaccustomed to leadership, he could not organize the marketing structure himself, and there was no one to do it for him. He wanted to return to life in the *ahupua'a* where he provided one commodity to the flow of goods, while others to whom he was related and whom he loved provided him with clothes and fish and pigs and *taro* and potatoes and all the other things he needed in life. These new ways were too much to understand. The upheaval in society was too much to take. He was lost. Buying land with its responsibilities was beyond him.[32]

The chiefs, in a different way, were also having their problems with capitalism. They were frequently inept at handling money and were almost always in debt. After the *mahele*, although they did not have money, they did have land. They passed the law in 1850 which allowed non-Hawaiian aliens to purchase property because they wanted to be able to sell their lands to pay existing debts and to buy more things. But this was like opening Pandora's Box. From then on, the chiefs were always in need of more and more money, and were forced to sell off more and more of their land.

While native Hawaiians may have been unaware of the great value of a clear land title, the white people in the islands, familiar with the capitalist system, were very aware of its value. They used their store of wealth to buy up every piece of land they could. By the end of 1850, the same year the law was passed allowing purchase of lands by anyone, thousands of acres had been sold to whites. Within two more years, the acreage sold would be in the hundreds of thousands. Before the monarchy came to an end forty years later, most of the chief's lands and vast parts of the crown lands and government lands had been sold to whites.[33]

> The 1890 census revealed the extent to which these forces had put land in the hands of the Westerners. Of a population near 90,000, fewer than 5,000 owned land. The relatively small number of Americans and Europeans owned more than one million acres. Three out of four acres belonging to private owners were held by Westerners.[34]

The worst fears of the thousands of native Hawaiians, who in the 1840s had petitioned the king not to grant private ownership, had come true.

Curiously, the American Board of Foreign Missions cut off support for the American missionaries in the islands during the same year that land first became available. The missionaries then petitioned the Privy Council, controlled at that time by whites, for land. Their petitions were made during the same months that the native Hawaiian commoners were securing title to the *kuleana*s they had claimed. In contrast to the small *kuleana*s being granted Hawaiian commoners—many between one and two acres—the white missionaries were granted 560 acres each at a nominal cost. "By 1855, forty-seven of the brethren had bought substantial lands amounting to thousands of acres."[35]

Having influenced the government to adopt private property, the missionaries, now cut off from support by the American mission board, turned to business. The following letter was written in 1851 by Rev. Amos Cooke, who had the year before begun a partnership with Rev. Samuel Castle. That partnership would grow into today's international conglomerate Castle and Cooke.

> "Here I am at my place of business and constantly interrupted by calls from the missionary brethren. At intervals I hope to be able to finish my correspondence that it may be in readiness for the "Overland" mail.
>
> It seems as if Providence was fighting against the nation internally.... Diseases are fast numbering the people with the dead, and many more are slow to take advantage of the times and of the privileges granted to them by the King and Government.... While the natives stand confounded and amazed at their privileges and doubting the truth of the changes on their behalf, the foreigners are creeping in among them, getting their largest and best lands, water privileges, building lots, etc., etc.
>
> The Lord seems to be allowing such things to take place that the Islands may gradually pass into other hands. This is trying, but we cannot help it. It is what we have been contending against for years, but the Lord is showing us that His thoughts are not our thoughts, neither are his ways our ways. The will of the Lord be done."[36]

And how better to comply with the new "will of the Lord" than to make sure the Lord's own missionaries and their families were first in line when lands began to pass into other hands.

Sugar: The White Takeover Continues

During the forty years between 1850 and 1890, the missionaries and their children, and other shrewd newcomers, put their future in sugar. They continued buying up lands from the chiefs, and they also bought and leased thousands of additional acres of the "government lands."

Business more and more became "the important thing" in the islands. But it was the white man's business: they owned the property. Sugar plantations grew large and powerful. The whole island economy came to depend on sugar. Whites imported Chinese, Japanese, and Portuguese to work in their fields, eventually bringing in sixty-one thousand immigrants.[37] With the new Asian immigrant population now so large, *haoles* who were landed or otherwise influential were a tiny part of the population indeed. But, given their position, they thought of themselves as masters of the uneducated, uncultured farm laborers. They also saw it as their place to completely dominate the Hawaiians. Newspapers of that time quote their repeated claims of superiority. These were **their** islands. And the islands and all of the people in them existed for them and for the pursuit of their wealth.[38]

In 1876 Hawai'i made a treaty of reciprocity with the United States which allowed Hawaiian sugar to be sold to America without paying import taxes. Reciprocity treaties could expire, however, and the first one did in 1883. The *haole* sugar growers in Hawai'i wanted a more permanent relationship that would guarantee exporting their sugar to the U.S. tax free. Annexation as a Territory of the United States would guarantee it. Many in the white community were American citizens who had never taken Hawaiian citizenship. Most of the other whites held at least dual citizenship with the United States. Thus, the greatest majority were predisposed for Annexation. A growing number thought of it as desirable if not immediately attainable.

In 1887, sugar interests were in trouble. It had been four years since the expiration of the first reciprocity treaty. The old treaty was being renewed on a year to year basis. The United States had not agreed to a new one. The U.S. had tried to get exclusive American use of Pearl Harbor put into the first treaty, but had been unsuccessful. Now the United States would not budge on a new treaty unless exclusive right to use of Pearl Harbor as a naval station was included. King Kalākaua refused, saying he would never ratify a treaty surrendering Pearl Harbor.

The island sugar producers, of course, wanted the treaty. After a newspaper campaign that attacked the king relentlessly on every front, the decent and responsible (i.e., almost entirely white and missionary descended) citizens of the kingdom formed a secret organization, the Hawaiian League.[39] Its members drew up a Constitution. In early July, the Honolulu Rifles, who were loyal to the Hawaiian League, took over Honolulu by armed force. While the Honolulu Rifles held the city, a delegation from the Hawaiian League forced King Kalākaua to sign their new constitution—which since that time has been referred to as the "Bayonet Constitution." It effectively stripped the king of most of his power. The House of Nobles, for instance, would be elected instead of appointed, and new voting requirements were so stringent and so carefully written that elections would be controlled by the white community. People the whites wanted would fill the House of Nobles. The House of Nobles would control the Cabinet. The Cabinet, according to the Constitution, would control the King. And the *haole* would have control of the kingdom.

After elections were held, when he no longer controlled the Legislature or the Cabinet, King Kalākaua, following the Constitutional requirement that he comply with the decisions of his Cabinet, signed the new reciprocity treaty giving America exclusive use of Pearl Harbor. For as long as the treaty would remain in force, that right would continue. The date was November 29, 1887.

It soon became obvious that the new reciprocity treaty was only a ploy to get Pearl Harbor. In 1891, less than four years after ratifying the treaty, Congress passed the McKinley Act allowing all the sugar of the world to enter the U.S. free of import duty. The United States had Pearl Harbor, but Hawaiian sugar no longer had any advantage over other foreign sugar. This crippled the Hawaiian sugar industry[40] and within a year caused a major depression in the islands.[41]

King Kalākaua died in 1891. His sister, Lili'uokalani, succeeded him. Within two years, her reign was toppled by the white business community and the American Minister with the support of American armed forces. The financial depression precipitated the overthrow. The planters and the business community were suffering great losses and the depression was getting worse each month. If Queen Lili'uokalani could be deposed and the islands annexed to the United States, sugar could be back "in the money" and the economy could rebound. For while the McKinley Act let all foreign sugar into the U.S. free of duty, it also provided a price support of two-cents per pound for domestic American sugar. If Hawai'i could become annexed to the United States, Hawaiian sugar would be domestic American sugar and could qualify for the two-cents per pound price support. Getting that price support, or some equivalent benefit, was a primary goal of the revolutionaries plotting the overthrow.[42]

Besides the depression, there was another reason for the overthrow. The *haole* community at this time comprised about 15% of the population. A small number in that *haole* community owned most of the land and ran most of the businesses. They needed to secure their possessions and their place of power against any possible confiscation by the larger population. Native Hawaiians wanted control of their government back. And they wanted their country back. Many in the white community supported the Hawaiian goals. The small clique in power was convinced that as long as a native Hawaiian monarch ruled, there was the possibility that they might lose everything they had. They were looking for some pretext to take over the government and annex the islands to the United States for their own security. The independent nation of the native Hawaiian people would be sacrificed to insure the economic advantage of a group primarily composed of children of the American missionaries who had come to save the Hawaiian people.

Quite soon after her accession to the throne, Queen Lili'uokalani received a petition signed by two-thirds of the citizens—mostly native Hawaiians—imploring her to do away with the Bayonet Constitution and to return the powers of government to the native Hawaiian citizens.[43]

In 1892, anticipating that the Queen would do away with the Bayonet Constitution—an act they could use as justification for her overthrow—members of the white community formed the Annexation Club. Unknown to the queen, Lorrin Thurston, one of the founders of the club, left for America where the Secretary of State and the Secretary of the Navy (speaking for President Harrison) gave Thurston encouraging words about Annexation should the overthrow take place.

When Thurston returned, he and the others in the Annexation Club waited for the chance for revolution. They met repeatedly with the American Minister plenipotentiary for Hawai'i, John L. Stevens. Stevens' letter of March 8, 1892—virtually setting out the course of the revolution—and his letter of November 20, 1892—calling for bold and vigorous measures for annexation—establish beyond question that he plotted with them for the overthrow.[44]

On January 14, 1893, Queen Lili'uokalani told her cabinet of her intention to adopt her newly finished Constitution. She was encouraged to wait for a few days by members of the cabinet who immediately took the news to the Annexation Club. A "Committee of Safety" was formed, composed of twelve members from the Annexation Club and one outsider. On the Committee, there were five Americans, six Hawaiian citizens by birth or naturalization (who also held dual citizenship from America), one Englishman, and one German. They resolved to proclaim a provisional government. "The queen herself, they said, had committed a revolutionary act when she proposed to alter the constitution, and this justified the 'intelligent part of the community' taking things into their own hands."[45]

Hearing of what was happening the Queen published word that she was formally laying aside her own constitution and committing herself to abide by the Bayonet Constitution. She also sent announcement of this formal declaration to all of the foreign ministers in Hawai'i, including the American minister.[46] Now there was no justification for the overthrow. But the Committee of Safety was not about to let that stop them.

Details of what happened in those few days are best told in the words of the President of the United States, Grover Cleveland. His "Message" to the Congress describing the situation will be quoted in its entirety as the next chapter.

To understand why Cleveland sent this Message to Congress, let us skip over the overthrow, and quickly describe the events which followed it. Thurston had been told on his trip to Washington in 1892 that if the overthrow took place, a proposition of annexation would find an extremely sympathetic administration under President Harrison.[47] However, after the overthrow, when representatives of the provisional government got to Washington seeking annexation, the administration of Benjamin Harrison was leaving office. A treaty of annexation was hurriedly negotiated, signed, and—within twelve days from the arrival of the Annexationist delegation in Washington D.C.—sent by President Harrison to the U.S. Senate for approval. But Grover Cleveland became President before the Senate acted. Cleveland withdrew the treaty from the Senate, and had an investigation into the situation conducted in Hawai'i by James H. Blount, the chairman of the Committee on Foreign Affairs in the House of Representatives.   After receiving Blount's report, Cleveland wrote the following Message to Congress describing the situation and explaining his actions.

Message

of

President Grover Cleveland
to the Congress

TO THE SENATE AND HOUSE OF REPRESENTATIVES:

In my recent annual message to the Congress I briefly referred to our relations with Hawaii and expressed the intention of transmitting further information on the subject when additional advices permitted.

Though I am not able now to report a definite change in the actual situation, I am convinced that the difficulties lately created both here and in Hawaii and now standing in the way of a solution, through Executive action, of the problem presented, render it proper, and expedient, that the matter should be referred to the broader authority and discretion of Congress, with a full explanation of the endeavor thus far made to deal with the emergency, and a statement of the considerations which have governed my actions.

I suppose that right and justice should determine the path to be followed in treating this subject. If national honesty is to be disregarded and a desire for territorial extension, or dissatisfaction with a form of government not our own, ought to regulate our conduct, I have entirely misapprehended the mission and character of our

Government and the behavior which the conscience of our people demands of our public servants.

When the present Administration entered upon its duties, the Senate had under consideration a treaty providing for the annexation of the Hawaiian Islands to the territory of the United States. Surely under our Constitution and laws the enlargement of our limits is a manifestation of the highest attribute of sovereignty, and if entered upon as an Executive act, all things relating to the transaction should be clear and free from suspicion. Additional importance attached to this particular treaty of annexation, because it contemplated a departure from unbroken American tradition in providing for the addition to our territory of islands of the sea more than two thousand miles removed from our nearest coast.

These considerations might not of themselves call for interference with the completion of a treaty entered upon by a previous Administration. But it appeared from the documents accompanying the treaty when submitted to the Senate, **that the ownership of Hawaii was tendered to us by a provisional government set up to succeed the constitutional ruler of the islands, who had been dethroned, and it did not appear that such provisional government had the sanction of either popular revolution or suffrage.** Two other remarkable features of the transaction naturally attracted attention. One was the extraordinary haste —not to say precipitancy— characterizing all the transactions connected with the treaty. It appeared that a so-called Committee of Safety, ostensibly the source of the revolt against the constitutional Government of Hawaii, was organized on Saturday, the 14th day of January; that on Monday, the 16th, the United States forces were landed at Honolulu from a naval vessel lying in its harbor; that on the 17th the scheme of a provisional government was perfected, and a proclamation naming its officers was on the same day prepared and read at the Government building; that immediatelly thereupon the United States Minister recognized the provisional government thus created; that two days afterward, on the 19th day of January, commissioners representing such government sailed for this country in a steamer especially chartered for the occasion, arriving in San Francisco on the 28th day of January, and in Washington on the 3d day of February; that on the next day they had their first interview with the Secretary of State, and another on the 11th, when the treaty of annexation was practically agreed upon, and that on the 14th it was formally concluded and on the 15th transmitted to the Senate. Thus between the initiation of the scheme for a provisional government in Hawaii on the 14th day of January and the submission to the Senate of the treaty of annexation concluded with such government, the entire interval was thirty-two days, fifteen of which were spent by the Hawaiian Commissioners in their journey to Washington.

In the next place, upon the face of the papers submitted with the treaty, it clearly appeared that there was open and undetermined an issue of fact of the most vital importance. The message of the President accompanying the treaty declared that the overthrow of the monarchy was not in any way promoted by this Government, and in a letter to the President from the Secretary of State, also submitted to the Senate with the treaty, the following passage occurs: "At the time the provisional government took possession of the Government buildings, no troops or officers of the United States were present or took any part whatever in the proceedings. No public recognition was accorded to the provisional government by the United States Minister until after the Queen's abdication, and when they were in effective possession of the Government buildings, the archives, the treasury, the barracks, the police station, and all the potential machinery of the Government." But a protest also accompanied said treaty, signed by the Queen and her ministers at the time she made way for the provisional government, which explicitly stated that she yielded to the superior force of the United States, whose Minister had caused United States troops to be landed at Honolulu and declared that he would support such provisional government.

The truth or falsity of this protest was surely of the first importance. If true, nothing but the concealment of its truth could induce our Government to negotiate with the semblance of a government thus created, nor could a treaty resulting from the acts stated in the protest have been knowingly deemed worthy of consideration by the Senate. Yet the truth or falsity of the protest had not been investigated.

I conceived it to be my duty therefore to withdraw the treaty from the Senate for examination, and meanwhile to cause an accurate, full, and impartial investigation to be made of the facts attending the subversion of the constitutional Government of Hawaii, and the installment in its place of the provisional government. I selected for the work of investigation the Hon. James H. Blount, of Georgia, whose service of eighteen years as a member of the House of Representatives, and whose experience as chairman of the Committee of Foreign Affairs in that body, and his consequent familiarity with international topics, joined with his high character and honorable reputation, seemed to render him peculiarly fitted for the duties entrusted to him. His report detailing his action under the instructions given to him and the conclusions derived from his investigation accompany this message.

These conclusions do not rest for their acceptance entirely upon Mr. Blount's honesty and ability as a man, nor upon his acumen and impartiality as an investigator. They are accompanied by the evidence upon which they are based, which evidence is also herewith transmitted, and from which it seems to me no other deductions could possibly be reached than those arrived at by the Commissioner.

The report with its accompanying proofs, and such other evidence as is now before the Congress or is herewith submitted, justifies in my opinion the statement that when the President was led to submit the treaty to the Senate with the declaration that "the overthrow of the monarchy was not in any way promoted by this Government", and when the Senate was induced to receive and discuss it on that basis, both President and Senate were misled.

The attempt will not be made in this communication to touch upon all the facts which throw light upon the progress and consummation of this scheme of annexation. A very brief and imperfect reference to the facts and evidence at hand will exhibit its character and the incidents in which it had its birth.

It is unnecessary to set forth the reasons which in January, 1893, led a considerable proportion of American and other foreign merchants and traders residing at Honolulu to favor the annexation of Hawaii to the United States. It is sufficient to note that fact and to observe that the project was one which was zealously promoted by the Minister representing the United States in that country. He evidently had an ardent desire that it should become a fact accomplished by his agency and during his ministry, and was not inconveniently scrupulous as to the means employed to that end. On the 19th day of November, 1892, nearly two months before the first overt act tending towards the subversion of the Hawaiian Government and the attempted transfer of Hawaiian territory to the United States, he addressed a long letter to the Secretary of State in which the case for annexation was elaborately argued, on moral, political, and economic grounds. He refers to the loss to the Hawaiian sugar interests from the operation of the McKinley bill, and the tendency to still further depreciation of sugar property unless some positive measure of relief is granted. He strongly inveighs against the existing Hawaiian Government and emphatically declares for annexation. He says: "In truth the monarchy here is an absurd anachronism. It has nothing on which it logically or legitimately stands. The feudal basis on which it once stood no longer existing, the monarchy now is only an impediment to good government—an obstruction to the prosperity and progress of the islands."

He further says: "As a crown colony of Great Britain or a Territory of the United States the government modifications could be made readily and good administration of the law secured. Destiny and the vast future interests of the United States in the Pacific clearly indicate who at no distant day must be responsible for the government of these islands. Under a territorial government they could be as easily governed as any of the existing Territories of the United States....Hawaii has reached the parting of the ways. She must now take the road which leads to Asia, or the other which outlets her in America, gives her an American civilization, and binds her to the care of American destiny." He also declares: "One of two courses seems to me absolutely necessary to be followed, either bold and vigorous measures for annexation or a 'customs union,' an ocean cable from the Californian coast to Honolulu, Pearl Harbor perpetually ceded to the United States, with an implied but not expressly stipulated American protectorate over the islands. I believe the former to be the better, that which will prove much the more advantageous to the islands, and the cheapest and least embarrassing in the end to the United States. If it was wise for the United States through Secretary Marcy thirty-eight years ago to offer to expend $100,000 to secure a treaty of annexation, it certainly can not be chimerical or unwise to expend $100,000 to secure annexation in the near future. To-day the United States has five times the wealth she possessed in 1854, and the reasons now existing for annexation are much stronger than they were then. I can not refrain from expressing the opinion with emphasis that the golden hour is near at hand."

These declarations certainly show a disposition and condition of mind, which may be usefully recalled when interpreting the significance of the Minister's conceded acts or when considering the probabilities of such conduct on his part as may not be admitted.

In this view it seems proper to also quote from a letter written by the Minister to the Secretary of State on the 8th day of March, 1892, nearly a year prior to the first step taken toward annexation. After stating the possibility that the existing Government of Hawaii might be overturned by an orderly and peaceful revolution, Minister Stevens writes as follows: "Ordinarily in like circumstances, the rule seems to be to limit the landing and movement of United States forces in foreign waters and dominion exclusively to the protection of the United States legation and of the lives and property of American citizens. But as the relations of the United States to Hawaii are exceptional, and in former years the United States officials here took somewhat exceptional action in circumstances of disorder, I desire to know how far the present Minister and naval commander may deviate from established international rules and precedents in the contingencies indicated in the first part of this dispatch."

To a minister of this temper full of zeal for annexation there seemed to arise in January, 1893, the precise opportunity for which he was watchfully waiting—an opportunity which by timely "deviation from established international rules and precedents" might be improved to successfully accomplish the great object in view: and we are quite prepared for the exultant enthusiasm with which in a letter to the State Department dated February 1, 1893, he declares: "The Hawaiian pear is now fully ripe and this is the golden hour for the United States to pluck it."

As a further illustration of the activity of this diplomatic representative, attention is called to the fact that on the day the above letter was written, apparently unable longer to restrain his ardor, he issued a proclamation whereby "in the name of the United States" he assumed the protection of the Hawaiian Islands and declared that said action was "taken pending and subject to negotiations at Washington." Of course this assumption of a protectorate was promptly disavowed by our Government, but the American flag remained over the Government building at Honolulu and the forces remained on guard until April, and after Mr. Blount's arrival on the scene, when both were removed.

A brief statement of the occurrences that led to the subversion of the constitutional Government of Hawaii in the interests of annexation to the United States will exhibit the true complexion of that transaction.

On Saturday, January 14, 1893, the Queen of Hawaii, who had been contemplating the proclamation of a new constitution, had, in deference to the wishes and remonstrances of her cabinet, renounced the project for the present at least. Taking this relinquished purpose as a basis of action, citizens of Honolulu numbering from fifty to one hundred, mostly resident aliens, met in a private office and selected a so-called Committee of Safety, composed of thirteen persons, seven of whom were foreign subjects, and consisted of five Americans, one Englishman, and one German. This committee, though its designs were not revealed, had in view nothing less than annexation to the United States, and between Saturday, the 14th, and the following Monday, the 16th of January—though exactly what action was taken may not be clearly disclosed—they were certainly in communication with the United States Minister. On Monday morning the Queen and her cabinet made public proclamation, with a notice which was specially served upon the representatives of all foreign governments, that any changes in the constitution would be sought only in the methods provided by that instrument. Nevertheless, at the call and under the auspices of the Committee of Safety, a mass meeting of citizens was held on that day to protest against the Queen's alleged illegal and unlawful proceedings and purposes. Even at this meeting the Committee of Safety continued to disguise their real purpose and contented themselves with procuring the passage of a resolution denouncing the Queen and empowering the committee to devise ways and means "to secure the permanent maintenance of law and order and the protection of life, liberty, and property in Hawaii."

This meeting adjourned between three and four o'clock in the afternoon. On the same day, and immediately after such adjournment, the committee, unwilling to take further steps without the cooperation of the United States Minister, addressed him a note representing that the public safety was menaced and that lives and property were in danger, and concluded as follows: "We are unable to protect ourselves without aid, and therefore pray for the protection of the United States forces." Whatever may be thought of the other contents of this note, the absolute truth of this latter statement is incontestable. **When the note was written and delivered, the committee, so far as it appears, had neither a man nor a gun at their command, and after its delivery they became so panic-stricken at their position that they sent some of their number to interview the Minister and request him not to land the United States forces till the next morning. But he replied that the troops had been ordered, and whether the committee were ready or not the landing should take place.** [Emphasis added]. And so it happened that on the 16th day of January, between four and five o'clock in the afternoon, a detachment of marines from the United States steamer Boston, with two pieces of artillery, landed at Honolulu. The men, upwards of 160 in all, were supplied with double cartridge belts filled with ammunition and with haversacks and canteens, and were accompanied by a hospital corps with stretchers and medical supplies. **This military demonstration upon the** soil of Honolulu was of itself an act of war, unless made either with the consent of the Government of Hawaii or for the *bona fide* purpose of protecting the imperilled lives and property of citizens of the United States. But there is no pretense of any such consent on the part of the Government of the Queen, which at the time was undisputed and was both the *de facto* and the *de jure* government. [Emphasis added.] In point of fact the existing government, instead of requesting the presence of an armed force, protested against it. There is as little basis for the pretense that such forces were landed for the security of American life and property. If so, they would have been stationed in the vicinity of such property and so as to protect it, instead of at a distance and so as to command the Hawaiian Government building and palace. Admiral Skerrett, the officer in command of our naval force on the Pacific station, has frankly stated that in his opinion the location of the troops was inadvisable if they were landed for the protection of American citizens whose residences and places of business, as well as the legation and consulate, were in a distant part of the city, but the location selected was a wise one if the forces were landed for the purpose of supporting the provisional government. If any peril to life and property calling for any such martial array had existed, Great Britain and other foreign powers interested would not have been behind the United States in activity to protect their citizens. But they made no sign in that direction. When these armed men were landed, the city of Honolulu was in its customary orderly and peaceful condition. There was no symptom of riot or disturbance in any quarter. Men, women, and children were about the streets as usual, and nothing varied the ordinary routine or disturbed the ordinary tranquillity, except the landing of the *Boston*'s marines and their march through the town to the quarters assigned them. Indeed, the fact that after having called for the landing of the United States forces on the plea of danger to life and property, the Committee of Safety themselves requested the Minister to postpone action, exposed the untruthfulness of their representations of present peril to life and property. The peril they saw was an anticipation growing out of guilty intentions on their part and something which, though not then existing, they knew would certainly follow their attempt to overthrow the Government of the Queen without the aid of the United States forces.

Thus it appears that Hawaii was taken possession of by the United States forces without the consent or wish of the government of the islands, or of anybody else so far as shown, except the United States Minister.

Therefore the military occupation of Honolulu by the United States on the day mentioned was wholly without justification, either as an occupation by consent or as an occupation necessitated by dangers threatening American life and property. [Emphasis added.] It must be accounted for in some other way and on some other ground, and its real motive and purpose are neither obscure nor far to seek.

The United States forces being now on the scene and favorably stationed, the committee proceeded to carry out their original scheme. They met the next morning, Tuesday, the 17th, perfected the plan of temporary government, and fixed upon its principal officers, ten of whom were drawn from the thirteen members of the Committee of Safety. Between one and two o'clock, by squads and by different routes to avoid notice, and having first taken the precaution of ascertaining whether there was any one there to oppose them, they proceeded to the Government building to proclaim the new government. No sign of oppostion was manifest, and thereupon an American citizen began to read the proclamation from the steps of the Government building almost entirely without auditors. It is said that before the reading was finished quite a concourse of persons, variously estimated at from 50 to 100, some armed and some unarmed, gathered about the committee to give them aid and confidence. This statement is not unimportant, since the one controlling factor in the whole affair was unquestionably the United States marines, who, drawn up under arms and with artillery in readiness only seventy-six yards distant, dominated the situation.

The provisional government thus proclaimed was by the terms of the proclamation "to exist until terms of union with the United States had been negotiated and agreed upon." The United States Minister, pursuant to prior agreement, recognized this government within an hour after the reading of the proclamation, and before five o'clock, in answer to an inquiry on behalf of the Queen and her cabinet, announced that he had done so.

When our Minister recognized the provisional government, the only basis upon which it rested was the fact that the Committee of Safety had in the manner above stated declared it to exist. It was neither a government *de facto* nor *de jure*. That it was not in such possession of the Government property and agencies as entitled it to recognition is conclusively proved by a note found in the files of the Legation at Honolulu, addressed by the declared head of the provisional government to Minister Stevens, dated January 17, 1893, in which he acknowledges with expressions of appreciation the Minister's recognition of the

provisional government, and states that it is not yet in the
possession of the station house (the place where a large
number of the Queen's troops were quartered), though the
same had been demanded of the Queen's officers in charge.
Nevertheless, this wrongful recognition by our Minister
placed the Government of the Queen in a position of most
perilous perplexity. On the one hand she had possession of
the palace, the barracks, and of the police station, and had at
her command at least five hundred fully armed men and
several pieces of artillery. Indeed, the whole military force
of her kingdom was on her side and at her disposal, while
the Committee of Safety, by actual search, had discovered
that there were but very few arms in Honolulu that were not
in the service of the Government. In this state of things, if
the Queen could have dealt with the insurgents alone her
course would have been plain and the result unmistakable.
But the United States had allied itself with her enemies, had
recognized them as the true Government of Hawaii, and had
put her and her adherents in the position of opposition
against lawful authority. She knew that she could not
withstand the power of the United States, but she believed
that she might safely trust to its justice. Accordingly, some
hours after the recognition of the provisional government by
the United States Minister, the palace, the barracks, and the
police station, with all the military resources of the country,
were delivered up by the Queen, upon the representation
made to her that her cause would thereafter be reviewed at
Washington, and while protesting that she surrendered to
the superior force of the United States, whose Minister had
caused United States troops to be landed at Honolulu and
declared that he would support the provisional government,
and that she yeilded her authority to prevent collision of
armed forces and loss of life and only until such time as the

United States, upon the facts being presented to it, should undo the action of its representative and reinstate her in the authority she claimed as the constitutional sovereign of the Hawaiian Islands.

This protest was delivered to the chief of the provisional government, who endorsed thereon his acknowledgement of its receipt. The terms of the protest were read without dissent by those assuming to constitute the provisional government, who were certainly charged with the knowledge that the Queen instead of finally abandoning her power had appealed to the justice of the United States for reinstatement in her authority; and yet the provisional government with this unanswered protest in its hand hastened to negotiate with the United States for the permanent banishment of the Queen from power and for a sale of her kingdom.

Our country was in danger of occupying the position of having actually set up a temporary government on foreign soil for the purpose of acquiring through that agency territory which we had wrongfully put in its possession. The control of both sides of a bargain acquired in such a manner is called by a familiar and unpleasant name when found in private transactions. We are not without a precedent showing how scrupulously we avoided such accusations in former days. After the people of Texas had declared their independence of Mexico they resolved that on the acknowledgement of their independence by the United States they would seek admission into the Union. Several months after the battle of San Jacinto, by which Texan independence was practically assured and and established, President Jackson declined to recognize it, alleging as one of his reasons that in the circumstances it became us "to beware of a too early movement, as it might subject us, however unjustly, to the imputation of seeking to establish the claim of our neighbors to a territory with a view to its subsequent acquisition by ourselves." This is in marked contrast with the hasty recognition of a government openly and concededly set up for the purpose of tendering to us territorial annexation.

I believe that a candid and thorough examination of the facts will force the conviction that the provisional government owes its existence to an armed invasion by the United States. Fair minded people with the evidence before them will hardly claim that the Hawaiian Government was overthrown by the people of the islands or that the provisional government had ever existed with their consent. I do not understand that any member of this government claims that the people would uphold it by their suffrages if they were allowed to vote on the question. [Emphasis added.]

While naturally sympathizing with every effort to establish a republican form of government, it has been the settled policy of the United States to concede to people of foreign countries the same freedom and independence in the management of their domestic affairs that we have always claimed for ourselves; and it has been our practice to recognize revolutionary governments as soon as it became apparent that they were supported by the people. For illustration of this rule I need only to refer to the revolution in Brazil in 1889, when our Minister was instructed to recognize the Republic "so soon as a majority of the people of Brazil should have signified their assent to its establishment and maintenance"; and to the revolution in Venzuela in 1892, when our recognition was accorded on condition that the new government was "fully established, in possession of the power of the nation, and accepted by the people."

As I apprehend the situation, we are brought face to face with the following conditions:

The lawful Government of Hawaii was overthrown without the drawing of a sword or the firing of a shot by a process every step of which, it may safely be asserted, is directly traceable to and dependent for its success upon the agency of the United States acting through its diplomatic and naval representatives.

But for the notorious predilections of the United States Minister for annexation, the Committee of Safety, which should be called the Committee of Annexation, would never have existed.

But for the landing of the United States forces upon false pretexts respecting the danger to life and property the committee would never have exposed themselves to the pains and penalties of treason by undertaking the subversion of the Queen's Government.

But for the presence of the United States forces in the immediate vicinity and in position to afford all needed protection and support, the committee would not have proclaimed the provisional government from the steps of the Government building.

And finally, but for the lawless occupation of Honolulu under false pretexts by the United States forces, and but for Minister Steven's recognition of the provisional government when the United States forces were its sole support and constituted its only military strength, the

Queen and her Government would never have yielded to the provisional government, even for a time and for the sole purpose of submitting her case to the enlightened justice of the United States.

Believing, therefore, that the United States could not, under the circumstances disclosed, annex the islands without justly incurring the imputation of acquiring them by unjustifiable methods, I shall not again submit the treaty of annexation to the Senate for its consideration, and in the instructions to Minister Willis, a copy of which accompanies this message, I have directed him to so inform the provisional government. [Emphasis added.]

But in the present instance our duty does not, in my opinion, end with refusing to consummate this questionable transaction. It has been the boast of our Government that it seeks to do justice in all things without regard to the strength or weakness of those with whom it deals. I mistake the American people if they favor the odious doctrine that there is no such thing as international morality, that there is one law for a strong nation and another for a weak one, and that even by indirection a strong power may with impunity despoil a weak one of its territory.

By an act of war committed with the participation of a diplomatic representative of the United States and without authority of Congress, the Government of a feeble but friendly and confiding people has been overthrown. A substantial wrong has thus been done which a due regard for our national character as well as the rights of the injured people requires we should endeavor to repair. [Emphasis added.] The provisional government has not assumed a republican or other constitutional form, but has remained a mere executive council or oligarchy, set up without the assent of the people. It has not sought to find a permanent basis of popular support and has given no evidence of an intention to do so. Indeed, the representatives of that government assert that the people of Hawaii are unfit for popular government and frankly avow that they can be best ruled by arbitrary or despotic power.

The law of nations is founded upon reason and justice, and the rules of conduct governing individual relations between citizens or subjects of a civilized state are equally applicable as between enlightened nations. The considerations that international law is without a court for its enforcement, and that obedience to its commands practically depends upon good faith, instead of upon the mandate of a superior tribunal, only give additional sanction to the law itself and brand any deliberate infraction of it not merely as a wrong but as a disgrace. A man of true honor protects the unwritten word which binds his conscience more scrupulously, if possible, than he does the bond a breach of which subjects him to legal liabilities; and the United States in aiming to maintain itself as one of the most enlightened of nations would do its citizens gross injustice if it applied to its international relations any other than a high standard of honor and morality. On that ground the United States can not properly be put in the position of countenancing a wrong after its commission any more than in that of consenting to it in advance. **On that ground it can not allow itself to refuse to redress an injury inflicted through an abuse of power by officers clothed with its authority and wearing its uniform; and on the same ground, if a feeble but friendly state is in danger of being robbed of its independence and its sovereignty by a**

misuse of the name and power of the United States, the United States can not fail to vindicate its honor and its sense of justice by an earnest effort to make all possible reparation. [Emphasis added.]

These principles apply to the present case with irresistible force when the special conditions of the Queen's surrender of her sovereignty are recalled. **She surrendered not to the provisional government, but to the United States. She surrendered not absolutely and permanently, but temporarily and conditionally until such time as the facts could be considered by the United States.** [Emphasis added.] Furthermore, the provisional government acquiesced in her surrender in that manner and on those terms, not only by tacit consent, but through the positive acts of some members of that government who urged her peaceable submission, not merely to avoid bloodshed, but because she could place implicit reliance upon the justice of the United States, and that the whole subject would be finally considered at Washington.

I have not, however, overlooked an incident of this unfortunate affair which remains to be mentioned. The members of the provisional government and their supporters, though not entitled to extreme sympathy, have been led to their present predicament of revolt against the Government of the Queen by the indefensible encouragement and assistance of our diplomatic representative. This fact may entitle them to claim that in our effort to rectify the wrong committed some regard should be had for their safety. This sentiment is strongly seconded by my anxiety to do nothing which would invite either harsh retaliation on the part of the Queen or violence and bloodshed in any quarter. In the belief that the Queen, as well as her enemies, would be willing to adopt such a course as would meet these conditions, and in view of the fact that both the Queen and the provisional government had at one time apparently acquiesced in a reference of the entire case to the United States Government, and considering the further fact that in any event the provisional government by its own declared limitation was only "to exist until terms of union with the United States of America have been negotiated and agreed upon," I hoped that after the assurance to the members of that government that such union could not be consummated I might compass a peaceful adjustment of the difficulty.

Actuated by these desires and purposes, and not unmindful of the inherent perplexities of the situation nor of the limitations upon my power, I instructed Minister Willis to advise the Queen and her supporters of my desire to aid in the restoration of the status existing before **the lawless landing of the United States forces at Honolulu** on the 16th of January last, if such restoration could be effected upon terms providing for clemency as well as justice to all parties concerned. The conditions suggested, as the instructions show, contemplate a general amnesty to those concerned in setting up the provisional government and a recognition of all its *bona fide* acts and obligations. In short, they require that the past should be buried, and that the restored Government should reassume its authority as if its continuity had not been interrupted. These conditions have not proved acceptable to the Queen, and though she has been informed that they will be insisted upon, and that, unless acceded to, the efforts of the President to aid in the restoration of her Government will cease, I have not thus far learned that she is willing to yield them her acquiescence.

The check which my plans have thus encountered has prevented their presentation to the members of the provisional government, while unfortunate public misrepresentations of the situation and exaggerated statements of the sentiments of our people have obviously injured the prospects of successful Executive mediation.

I therefore submit this communication with its accompanying exhibits, embracing Mr. Blount's report, the evidence and statements taken by him at Honolulu, the instructions given to both Mr. Blount and Minister Willis, and correspondence connected with the affair in hand.

In commending this subject to the extended powers and wide discretion of the Congress, I desire to add the assurance that I shall be much gratified to cooperate in any legislative plan which may be devised for the solution of the problem before us which is consistent with American honor, integrity, and morality.

GROVER CLEVELAND

Executive Mansion,
Washington, December 18, 1893

Hawai'i Under Non-Hawaiian Rule

IN THE MIDDLE OF DECEMBER, 1893, just about the time that President Cleveland's "Message" was given to Congress, Lili'uokalani did agree to an amnesty for the members of the provisional government. Minister Willis of the United States took her decision to the Provisional Government and asked if now they would restore the monarchy in accordance with President Cleveland's wishes. The answer was "No." Their argument was that they were now a government themselves, that they had been recognized by America and by other great powers as **the** government for the Hawaiian Islands, and that they would not allow President Cleveland and the American government to "interfere in the internal affairs of their sovereign nation."[1]

President Cleveland had closed his "Message" by giving Congress control over a solution to the problem. When Congress was pressed for a decision, they opted for inaction. Despite the clear case presented by the President of immoral and illegal wrongdoing by the United States in the setting up of this hollow, non-representative government, now that the situation was so favorable to American interests, Congress conveniently decided they should follow the precepts of international law and not interfere in the "internal affairs" of the "sovereign government" of Hawai'i. The provisional government was allowed to stay in power.

Like Kamehameha III before her, in his experience with Britain, the Queen had depended on the justice of a great nation to restore her throne.   Unlike Britain, however, America found greed a stronger passion than justice.

The provisional government began to take steps to establish itself as a permanent government. Sanford Dole, the president, announced an election for delegates to a Constitutional Convention. But, making sure that the new constitution would reflect the goals of the revolutionaries, nineteen delegates were appointed by Dole himself, and only eighteen were elected. To vote, one had to sign an oath declaring allegiance to the new regime and swearing to oppose any attempt to restore the monarchy.   This, of course, prevented most native Hawaiians from voting. Even among the white people, however, voting for delegates was very light.[2]

Qualifications for future voting were even more stringent when the new constitution emerged. Men had to own property, swear allegiance to the Republic and swear to oppose the restoration of the monarchy; they also had to be able to speak, read, and write English, and be able to explain the constitution—**which was written in English**—to the satisfaction of members of the government.

Once the new constitution was completed, it was time for a vote to adopt it and thus to establish the Republic of Hawai'i. However, as Gavan Daws notes, in the opinion of the provisional government even those few thousand voters who had elected the delegates to write the constitution could not be trusted to endorse it, and so the constitution became law not by plebiscite but by proclamation. When Lili'uokalani intended to establish a new constitution by her own royal proclamation, even though she had the support of two-thirds of the voters, the revolutionaries declared her act to be so criminal that it justified their overthrow of the monarchy.　Now, fearing they could not count on the support of even their own backers, these same revolutionaries did what they overthrew the Queen for threatening to do: they established their own Constitution by proclamation.

"Sanford Dole announced the inauguration of the Republic of Hawai'i and proclaimed himself president on Fourth of July, 1894."[3] The significance of the date was lost on no one.

In that same year the United States Congress repealed the McKinley Act which had caused the depression and the overthrow of the monarchy.　The price support on sugar produced in the United States was removed, a new tariff was placed on sugar from other countries, and Hawaiian sugar was restored to its privileged place in the American market.[4]

An Analysis of the American Role in the Overthrow

One must ask why the McKinley Act of 1890 was ever passed.　Why would America tax its own economy voluntarily, instituting a huge price support for its domestic sugar while giving up all the import tax money it had been collecting on foreign sugar?　The whole thing doesn't seem to make good economic sense.　It becomes even more inexplicable when it is seen that passing the Act meant turning America's back on Hawai'i and precipitating a disastrous depression in the islands at a time when the United States had just acquired such a plum—Pearl Harbor—through negotiation of the 1887 sugar treaty with

Hawai'i. It is equally puzzling why this disastrous Act was in effect for only four years, and why its provisions were rescinded once the Annexationists were clearly in power and America's eventual possession of Hawai'i was assured.

There is strong evidence to indicate that the principal purpose for putting the sugar provisions of the McKinley Act into law was to topple the Hawaiian monarchy and to bring the islands under American control.

To really understand how America could be so involved, to understand how, over decades, it could have intentionally evolved a plan to engineer the overthrow, one must understand the mood and aspirations of America in the 1800s.   Consider carefully the history of America's colonialistic activity.   From its earliest years as a nation, America experienced an expansionist fervor.   Thomas Jefferson, the writer of the Declaration of Independence and third president of the United States—in a secret deal which Congress knew nothing about until they were asked to pay the bill—doubled the territory of the United States over-night by buying almost one-third of the American continent from the French in the Louisiana Purchase.[5] That was in 1803, sixteen years before the American missionaries left for Hawai'i.   This is only one example of young America's lust for lands.   Between 1810 and 1819, also before the missionaries' departure, America had fought the battle of New Orleans and taken the Spanish-held area west of it; it had also taken all of Florida from the Spanish; and Americans were poised and ready for their 1821 push into Texas.[6]

Were the American missionaries who came to Hawai'i in those years a part of this expansionist movement?

Researching the American Board of Commissioners for Foreign Missions, which sent the missionaries, one finds that besides the spiritual leaders, its principal backers were famous politicians: men at one time governors of Connecticut, New York, and New Hampshire; Congressmen; even a U.S. Secretary of State for Foreign Affairs. Other backers were men who had made fortunes in merchandising and shipping, whose lives centered around expanding American horizons and boundaries.[7] The missionaries were not only sent by this American Mission Board; they were supported by them and kept in close contact with them.

For America the missionaries would serve as goodwill ambassadors, as listening posts in the Pacific, as opinion shapers, as powerful pro-American influences, and as openers of markets. This is not to say that the missionaries intended to do anything other than sacrifice their lives to save the souls of the heathen Hawaiians, and in the process to give the Hawaiians "better lives." Their ideological colonialism destroyed the Hawaiian nation, however, with their insisting on Western-style private property until they forced the *mahele* into reality, and then their buying up and leasing large tracts of land until they or their children owned or controlled all the major business interests in the islands.

While this was happening in Hawai'i, the American nation was expanding westward and developing the philosophy of "Manifest Destiny" to support its imperialism. As America stretched westward, it found indigenous peoples in its way. What was to happen to them? Early cowboy and Indian movies tell the story from the American viewpoint quite accurately. The Americans were a rising people. By contrast, the Indian was necessarily a no-account, a trouble-maker, a problem standing in the way. Indians had to be conquered and either moved or wiped out. This was good and necessary. This attitude was not encountered occasionally and by chance as a solution to a specific cowboy and Indian problem here or there. Rather, it was the carefully formulated official policy of the U.S. government regarding native Americans: according to the doctrine of "Manifest Destiny," white Americans must fulfill their "Manifest Destiny allotted by Providence" to develop and rule the breadth of the continent. All actions to remove obstacles that stood in their way were therefore morally righteous, including the dispossession and slaughter of Indians.[8]

If the doctrine of "Manifest Destiny" was popular among the masses, it was even more fervidly embraced by those who were making that destiny fact—those in the military and the government.

As the years went on, the value of Hawai'i had become more and more obvious, not only to America, but to other colonial powers also, the British and the French. The Navy and the State Department began to plan ways to secure their ties to the islands.

It is hard to pinpoint the beginning of actual American meddling in the Hawaiian governmental activity. When Kamehameha V died in 1872, Admiral Pennock was sent to Honolulu with the following instructions:

> Go to Honolulu as soon as possible,...and in concert with [Minister Pierce], use all your influence and all proper means to direct and maintain feeling in favor of United States, and at least to secure selection of successor favorable to our interests.[9]

Lunalilo, who was favorable to America, had been elected king before Pennock arrived, and there was no need for America's interference. But aboard the same ship were Major General John M. Schofield, Commander of the U.S. Army Pacific, and Brigadier General B.S. Alexander of the Corps of Engineers, arriving on secret mission for the U.S. government. According to confidential orders from Secretary of War, W.W. Belknap, they were to visit the Hawaiian islands

> for the purpose of ascertaining the defensive capabilities of the different ports and their commercial facilities, and to examine into any other subjects that may occur to you as desirable, in order to collect all information that would be of service to the country in the event of war with a powerful maritime nation....It is believed the objects of this visit to the Sandwich Islands will be best accomplished, if your visit is regarded as a pleasure excursion, which may be joined in by your citizen friends.[10]

Schofield and Alexander stayed in Hawai'i two months. Touring the islands, they were shown its lush mountains and valleys and its gorgeous beaches, but their colonialist eyes saw only future militarily strategic bases—one at the only large natural harbor in the northern Pacific. Returning to the U.S. in 1873, they "subsequently prepared a report, made public twenty years later, which emphasized the value of Pearl Harbor and discussed the means of making it available for naval and commercial purposes."[11] Thus began the intense American interest in securing Pearl Harbor.

Hawai'i was interested in securing a reciprocity treaty with the United States. Among other things, such a treaty would greatly help the sugar interests. The American navy tried to secure a foothold in Pearl Harbor during negotiations for the treaty. This caused the negotiations to drag on; King Lunalilo died; and his successor Kalākaua was strongly opposed to cession of the harbor in any way, even leasing. He was successful in holding the admirals at bay. The first Reciprocity Treaty, signed in 1876, did, however, prohibit the Kingdom from leasing or otherwise disposing of any port, harbor, or territory to any power other than America during the treaty period.[12] Senator John T. Morgan of Alabama later wrote about the 1876 treaty, "The Hawaiian treaty was negotiated for the purpose of securing political control of those islands, making them industrially and commercially, a part of the United States."[13]

After the treaty of 1876, America began to take a more active role in guiding the internal politics of Hawai'i. In 1887 when the Hawaiian League and the Honolulu Rifles took over the city and forced Kalākaua to sign the bayonet constitution, the Hawaiian minister to Washington, H.A.P. Carter, although sent there by the king, convinced the Secretary of State to support the revolutionaries against the king. A letter from Carter's son, Charles, to Secretary of State Bayard tells the story:

> In June 1887, my father...came to...Michigan to attend my graduation...He was compelled to leave in the midst of the festivities because...he learned that it was the intention of the United States Government to send the warship Adams to Honolulu to protect the late King Kalākaua and his government from the anticipated Revolution predicted in the then latest dispatches and **he further told me that in consequence of his assurances to you, that the revolution was being conducted by his friends and would be in the best interests of Hawai'i, that the orders to [U.S.] Minister Merrill and the warships at Honolulu were not to interfere with those conducting the revolt.**[14] [Emphasis added.]

Following this move to withold support for the king in the revolution, the United States then pushed for exclusive rights to maintain a coaling station at Pearl Harbor, demanding that this be a part of the second Reciprocity Treaty in 1887.

The U.S. was successful this time. The power of Kalākaua being severely limited by the new Bayonet Constitution, he was forced to sign the treaty of 1887 granting America exclusive use of Pearl Harbor. This right would end, however, when the reciprocity treaty expired.

The Admirals of the American navy were growing in power. It was the eve of their spectacular victories in the Spanish-American War when Admiral Dewey would take the Philippines. Pearl Harbor had long been recognized as crucial to the Navy in order to promote and maintain American interests in the Pacific. The Congress, bowing to pressure from the Navy, had attempted to make use of Pearl Harbor a pre-condition for agreement to both the 1876 and the 1887 sugar Reciprocity Treaties. Perhaps the Navy could again use sugar as its tool in securing complete control over Pearl Harbor.

The McKinley Act was convenient. There were very few states producing sugar at that time. Opposition in Congress would not be strong. And the Congressmen from the sugar states could take home to their growers a two cents per pound price support to offset any losses. Such an Act would cause enough major problems in Hawai'i that the Annexationists would have "just cause" to overthrow the Queen. Hawai'i could then be annexed. And Pearl Harbor would then belong forever to the American naval forces.

That is the scenario. Are there additional facts to support it? First of all, the McKinley Act was no surprise when it took effect in 1891. The Hawaiian government had heard talk about it in 1888, within weeks after signing the reciprocity treaty with its lease of Pearl Harbor.[15] It certainly must be seen as strange that the United States government would sign a treaty protecting Hawaiian sugar interests and within a few weeks would be discussing a bill that would cripple it. The question must be asked, "When the United States was negotiating the treaty, did they ever really intend to protect Hawaiian sugar? Or was the treaty just another effort to secure Pearl Harbor for the Navy?

It seems that after the treaty was signed, when the Navy was not completely happy with the impermanence of what they got, they did decide to continue using the needs of the sugar industry to get more. Congress quickly started debating a bill that would threaten Hawaiian sugar and the Hawaiian economy with disaster, so the State Department would have leverage to push the government of Hawai'i into a permanent pact securing Pearl Harbor. During these next two years, 1888-89, the U.S. Secretary of State, James G. Blaine, attempted to negotiate two treaty proposals with the Hawaiian Minister. Both would have superseded the sugar provisions in the McKinley Act and given all Hawaiian products identical treatment with domestic American products. Both treaties also would have "guaranteed" the independence of the kingdom. This "guaranteeing" would have included a permanent American guard—which would have in effect also guaranteed the Navy permanent use of Pearl Harbor. The first treaty proposal also included "the landing of troops for this purpose if necessary." Although King Kalākaua's white annexationist cabinet urged agreement with both treaties, he realized that the native Hawaiians would be enraged over his making Hawai'i a protectorate of the U.S., and he refused to sign either.[16] The Reciprocity Treaty granting temporary use of the harbor was as far as he would go. He could not be budged.

If the king would not cooperate, said some, then get rid of the king, and the kingdom along with him. There were forces in the islands who wanted annexation. Give them a true rallying cause for an overthrow: a pain where it would hurt those who could be rallied most—in the pocketbook. The McKinley Act was signed into law by President Harrison in 1891. And the terrible economic depression began.

In 1892, the white annexationist leader, Lorrin Thurston, secretly visited Washington to search for support for Annexation should he and his small band of revolutionaries be able to overthrow the Queen. Thurston's *Memoirs of the Hawaiian Revolution* tell the fascinating story:

> Mr. Blaine [the Secretary of State] asked, "Have you talked to anyone else in Washington on this subject?" I answered that I had, mentioning Senator Davis and Mr. Blount.
> Mr. Blaine said that he considered the subject of the utmost importance, and continued, "I am somewhat unwell, but I wish you would call on B.F. Tracy, secretary of the navy, and tell him what you have told me, and say to him that I think you should see the President. Do not see Mr. Blount again. I will attend to him. Come to me after you have seen President Harrison." In accordance with the request, I immediately met Secretary Tracy and reported my conversation with Mr. Blaine.
> Said Mr. Tracy: "I do not know whether you had better see the President or not. But come with me, and we will learn what he thinks." We went to the White House. Mr. Tracy had me wait in an outer room while he spoke

with the President. After about a half-hour, the Secretary
reappeared and beckoned me to accompany him
outdoors. Then he spoke: "I have explained fully to the
President what you have said to me, and have this to say
to you: **the President does not think he should see you,
but he authorizes me to say to you that, if conditions in
Hawai'i compel you to act as you have indicated, and
you come to Washington with an annexation
proposition, you will find an exceedingly sympathetic
administration here."** That was all I wanted to know.[17]
[Emphasis added.]

After Thurston returned home, the economic depression
continued to worsen.   The American Minister, John L.
Stevens, who had been appointed by President Harrison and
was privy to all the communications between the President,
the Secretary of the Navy, and Thurston, acted in the
manner he knew his government at the time wanted him to
act.   Stevens joined with the revolutionaries and plotted
their revolution with them, as his letter of March 8, 1892,
shows.   He called in the American troops when the time
came, and he refused to call off the landing of the Marines
when the Committee of Safety got cold feet.   By doing this,
Stevens, the American Minister, **forced** the revolutionaries
to complete the overthrow.

The actions of the American Minister, John L. Stevens, are
said by many to be the individual actions of an over-zealous
minister, working alone and without the consent of the U.S.
government.   Such claims ignore the reality that Minister
John L. Stevens and James C. Blaine, Secretary of State
during the Harrison administration, had been close
friends—sharing the same aspirations and championing the
same causes—for thirty-seven years, when Blaine sent him
to be American Minister in Hawai'i.   As far back as 1854,
they had purchased and together edited a newspaper, the

Kennebec Journal, in Augusta, Maine. Together they had worked hard to promote and develop the Republican party in that state.[18]

Another close friend and political mentor to Stevens, Luther Severance, had been editor of the *Kennebec Journal* for twenty-five years when in 1850 he was appointed United States Minister to Hawai'i. He served in that post for two years. Severance supported annexation and, along with Blaine, greatly influenced Stevens' views "on the 'manifest destiny' of the United States in the Pacific region."[19]

Over the years, Secretary of State Blaine himself had made no secret of his support for annexation of Hawai'i.[20] In 1881, ten years before sending Stevens to Hawai'i, he had spoken of "the necessity of:

> drawing the ties of intimate relationship between us and
> the Hawaiian islands so as to make them practically a
> part of the American system without derogation of their
> absolute independence....If they drift from their
> independent station it must be toward assimilation and
> identification with the American system, to which they
> belong by the operation of natural laws and must belong
> by the operation of political necessity."[21]

Thus in 1891, when Blaine called upon Stevens, his close friend whom for almost forty years he had known to share his views and aspirations, and sent him to be American Minister to Hawai'i, Blaine knew that Stevens could be depended on to accomplish what the Secretary of State and the American President wanted done.[22] As Kuykendall concludes, "Stevens apparently thought it was his mission to see that the island kingdom did not stray from the path of its American destiny."[23]

Given all of these facts, there can be little argument that the United States did condone and support Stevens' activities as he planned and plotted the revolution with the annexationists and then forced the revolutionaries to go through with it.

For far more years than has even been imagined in the century since, America was involved in planning a takeover of Hawai'i—in the 1876 Reciprocity Treaty when America insisted on guarantees that no lease or sale of ports or lands could be made to other governments, in the bayonet revolution when America sided with the revolutionaries and witheld support for the King, in the 1878 Treaty of Reciprocity when America demanded and got exclusive use of Pearl Harbor, in the pressuring for two new treaties in 1888-89 that would permanently lease Pearl Harbor to the Navy, in moving ahead with the McKinley Act that caused the depression, in sending Stevens—who would carry out the Harrison Administration's view of "manifest destiny"—to be the American Minister to Hawai'i, in holding highest level Washington meetings with the annexationist leader Lorrin Thurston, in Stevens' planning the revolt with the annexationists, and finally in Stevens' eventual forcing the annexationists to carry through when they wanted postponement.   These facts support the Hawaiian claim that America had a clear history of meddling in the internal affairs of the sovereign Hawaiian nation, and that the American government conspired to overthrow the Hawaiian monarchy and supported the actual takeover with its troops.

President Cleveland, inaugurated two months after the overthrow of the monarchy, was a political enemy of former President Harrison, and very possibly knew nothing of the involvement of Harrison, Secretary of State James G. Blaine, Secretary of the Navy B.F. Tracy, Minister Stevens, and certain members of the Congress in the whole affair. When, however, during his administration he gave Congress the opportunity to solve the problem, those in power were not about to resist plucking the pear they had nurtured over the years to such ripeness. The provisional government would stay in power.

Later, when the revolutionaries were solidly entrenched and committed to the path of annexation, the provisions of the McKinley Act were repealed. It had only taken four years from its original passage: Pearl Harbor and the rest of Hawai'i would now belong to the United States forever.

When Sanford B. Dole was inaugurated as the first Territorial governor in 1900, a huge banner stretching the length of the balcony beneath him appropriately read, "Westward the course of empire...."[24]

Resistance by Native Hawaiians

What was the native Hawaiian sentiment towards all these happenings? Did native Hawaiians just go along? Or did they protest? Shortly after the Bayonet Constitution had been forced upon King Kalākaua in 1887, native Hawaiians formed a resistance. Robert Wilcox, a half-Hawaiian, who had been sent by Kalākaua to study politics in Italy, led an insurrection to reestablish the power of the king and to do away with the Bayonet Constitution. His troops were defeated. Seven Hawaiians were killed, and a dozen or so wounded. Wilcox was tried for high treason, but an all-Hawaiian jury acquitted him, and he became a national hero.[25] During the short reign of Queen Lili'uokalani, again Hawaiians under Wilcox plotted to take over the government and to save the islands for Hawaiians. Wilcox and other leaders were arrested but, because of their popularity, were never tried.[26]

With the monarchy overthrown, in 1895 Wilcox, having joined forces with Lili'uokalani, once more led an attempt to restore Hawaiian rule. Skirmishes went on for about ten days before the royalists surrendered. After they surrendered, to save them from death, Queen Lili'uokalani formally abdicated her throne. No one was sentenced to death. The Queen was imprisoned in the palace. She was the last of the prisoners to be released.[27]

The native Hawaiian community had spoken with its blood. It clearly did not want annexation to the United States.[28] Hawaiians continued to speak out against it. In 1897 they sent the so-called "monster petition," signed by 29,000 native Hawaiians, to the Congress protesting annexation.[29]

Annexation

In his Message to the Congress, President Cleveland had stated that the provisional government clearly did not represent the citizens of Hawai'i and therefore, according to international law, could not legally tender Hawai'i to the U.S. Five years later, ignoring international law, the U.S. accepted Hawai'i from that very same non-representative government, an action the President himself had judged as criminal.

After Grover Cleveland left office in 1897 and William McKinley was inaugurated as President of the United States, the Republic of Hawai'i sent another delegation to Washington to negotiate a treaty. President McKinley signed the Treaty of Annexation with the Republic of

Hawai'i on June 16, 1897. It then needed ratification by both countries. Hawai'i was no problem: the Senate of the Republic of Hawai'i ratified it on September 9, again without the matter ever having been brought before the people for a vote.

Ratification by the United States Senate would be more difficult. The Constitution of the United States explicitly states that all treaties must be ratified by two-thirds of the members of the Senate. This treaty did not have the required support in the U.S. Senate, so it was never ratified. Rather, it was laid aside in favor of an alternative move. Admission of Texas into the Union in 1845 had been accomplished through a joint resolution requiring only a majority vote in both houses of Congress. This avoided treaty ratification. A similar bill to annex Hawai'i was introduced. It was called the Newlands Resolution. Getting it through both houses of the Congress was no easy task, either. However, on May 1, 1898 Captain George Dewey sank the Spanish fleet in Manila harbor. Americans could see the value of holding on to the Philippines, and Hawai'i was seen as central to that move. Already passed by the Senate, the resolution for Annexation was quickly passed by the House and was signed by President McKinley on July 7, 1898.[30]

Formal annexation ceremonies took place in the islands on August 12, 1898. The Republic of Hawai'i would now be the Territory of Hawai'i, a Territory of the United States. The white community was deliriously happy. Native Hawaiians were desperately gloomy. The ceremony proclaiming the islands the Territory of Hawai'i took place in front of 'Iolani Palace, which had been renamed "Government Building." As Gavan Daws writes,[31] "The

Hawaiian anthem, 'Hawai'i Ponoi,' was played for the last time as the anthem of an independent nation, and the Hawaiian flag was hauled down. The Stars and Stripes took its place, and the band played 'The Star Spangled Banner.' 'To the Hawaiian born, it was pathetic,' wrote the *Pacific Commercial Advertiser*. This was the ultimate dispossession."

During the next two years, a constitution for the Territory of Hawai'i was hammered out and approved by Congress. That constitution is referred to as the Organic Act. It took effect on June 14, 1900, and lasted—with occasional changes made by Congress—until admission to Statehood August 21, 1959.[32]

The Ceded Lands

Earlier we read of the "crown lands" and the "government lands" which were set aside by King Kamehameha III at the time of the *mahele*. When the provisional government toppled the monarchy, they claimed that what remained of both sets of lands belonged to the new government. They then sold large portions of the lands during their few years of rule. There were protests at that time that the crown lands belonged to the Queen, and that the government lands were given in perpetuity to the native Hawaiian people, not to others living in Hawai'i. At annexation, however, both sets of lands were "ceded" to the United States by the Republic of Hawai'i, with the stipulation that they were to be held in trust for "the Hawaiian people." Since that time, these lands have been called the "Ceded Lands." They comprise about half of the land of the eight major islands. Native Hawaiians were never asked for permission to cede their lands to the United States, and they have never surrendered their claim to them as lands belonging specifically to native Hawaiians. During the years of the Territory, almost 20% of these lands were dedicated for federal use—143,700 acres for military bases and 227,972 acres for national parks.[33] Another 200,000 acres were set aside for homesteading by native Hawaiians through the Hawaiian Homes Act. At the time of admission to the Union in 1959, the rest of these lands were given to the State of Hawai'i to be held in trust for the Hawaiian and native Hawaiian people.

The native Hawaiian people today still lay claim to the entire territory included in the original Ceded Lands. And it is these lands, at a minimum, they want returned to their rule.

The Hawaiian Homes Commission Act

The native Hawaiians' right to the Ceded Lands was recognized by the Hawaiian Territorial government and by the American government in the events surrounding the Hawaiian Homes Act.

Twenty years after annexation, through the efforts of Prince Jonah Kūhiō Kalaniana'ole, who was the Territory's delegate to Congress at the time, some 200,000 acres of the "crown lands" and "government lands" which had been ceded to the United States at the time of annexation were formed into a special land trust for homesteading by native Hawaiians. This was brought about by the Hawaiian Homes Commission Act which was passed in 1921.

It had been recognized for many years that the Hawaiian people were not assimilating into Western society, and also that the Hawaiian race was fast disappearing. These had been persistent problems for nearly a century. One of the motivations for the *mahele,* seventy years earlier, had been to get native Hawaiians out of the slums in the towns and back onto the land. In the period just prior to 1920, people in Honolulu and in Washington were saying it aloud again: if the Hawaiians were to survive as a culture and as a race, they had to get back to the land and to reestablish their ties with nature. Congressional discussions of the proposed Act said it would "save the Hawaiian people from extinction by returning them to the land and to 'the mode of living that their ancestors were accustomed to.'"[34] Return of the trust lands to native Hawaiians would "rehabilitate" the people by giving them farms where they could be self-sufficient, where they could practice initiative, and where they could preserve their native Hawaiian culture.[35]

This was supportive talk, and it did get the bill passed. But, in reality the Hawaiian Homes Act came about as a response to plantation events rather than Hawaiian needs. There was very little that was noble about the intentions of many who were its strongest supporters in Hawai'i. Between 1915 and 1920, the plantations had 213,000 acres of the islands planted in sugar cane. Most of this acreage they owned outright. But 34,000 acres of their prime agricultural lands were "government lands" which they had leased from the government over the years.[36] The Organic Act, the Constitution for the new Territory of Hawai'i, had set a ceiling for the acreage of land that could be held by any single party in the Territory. That ceiling was 1000 acres per individual or corporation. For years the plantations had gotten around the 1000 acre limit by forming bogus partnerships or corporations. This was easy enough to do, with governors who were friendly to sugar. But there was always the worry that they might be taken to court where, if the circumvention were properly attacked, they knew that they would be beaten.[37] Sugar needed Section 55, with its thousand-acre ceiling, repealed from the Organic Act, the constitution of the Territory of Hawai'i.

Sugar also had another problem: homesteading. Provisions in the Organic Act allowed Hawaiians to homestead prime "government lands" leased by the sugar plantations, but governors friendly to sugar had consistently renewed expiring leases on the sugar acreage instead of opening up the good sugar lands for homesteading. Further, the plantations had such control over supplies, transportation, and marketing that they could easily drive those farmers who did succeed in getting homesteads out of business and off their lands.[38]

In an effort by Congress to encourage the Territory to open up leased lands for homesteading, the Organic Act was amended in 1908 to require that all leases on agricultural lands read that "at any time during the term of the lease [the property could] be withdrawn from operation for homesteading or public purposes." A year later, an even more radical change was made in the Organic Act: it encouraged groups of twenty-five or more people to get together and apply to homestead public property, and it obliged the Commission of Public Lands to open areas of prime agricultural land leased by the sugar plantations for homesteading.[39] This was a major cause for worry on the plantation. If a governor should be appointed now who was not friendly to sugar, he could use the withdrawal clause to open up any public lands for homesteading.

Sugar was in trouble. The mission boys, as the leadership in the Territory liked to call themselves, came up with a proposal for Prince Kūhiō, the delegate to Congress who for years had been pressing for the opening of homestead lands. If he agreed to allow the Organic Act to be changed in a way to keep homesteaders off of the sugar lands and also to delete the thousand-acre ownership ceiling, they would lobby Congress to set aside 200,000 acres of the Ceded Lands for homesteading by Native Hawaiians. Land already being used for cultivating sugar would be excluded from these homestead lands.   Forest preserves and lands already occupied by homesteaders under previous agreements would also be excluded.   Besides lobbying for the 200,000 acres for homesteads, the mission boys would agree that 30% of the revenues which the territory collected in lease rents from the "government lands" it leased to the plantations would be put into a fund for rehabilitation of the Hawaiian people.   Revenues would continue to be put into the fund until it reached one million dollars.   This "Home Loan Fund" was to be a fund from which native Hawaiian homesteaders could make loans to "erect buildings, purchase live stock and farm equipment, and otherwise assist in the development of tracts."[40]

The deal must have looked good to Prince Kūhiō. For years he had fought for homestead rights for his people, but friends of sugar in high places had thwarted him at every turn. He had met with almost total lack of success for so long, and there was no reason to expect anything different in the future. This deal at least guaranteed lands and money for his people.

But what native Hawaiians actually got was not much. Once sugar and forest lands were excluded from consideration, "what was left was land that no one had ever been able to make productive."[41]

For example, on the island of Maui the greatest part of the lands given to the Hawaiians for homesteading are on the desert side of Haleakalā volcano and rise up to the 9000 foot peak—beyond the timberline, beyond the vegetation line: Hawaiians were given lands to cultivate that were so high that in the entire history of the universe no plant has ever been able to survive and grow there. On the island of O'ahu, they were given hundreds of acres on the face of sheer, thousand-foot cliffs behind Waimānalo. Also on O'ahu they got the desert land of Nānākuli, thirty miles from town on the Wai'anae coast. One tradition says that Nānākuli, which means "Look at the deaf one," got its name because those who lived there had so little water that they pretended they were deaf when travellers passed through, so that they wouldn't have to offer traditional hospitality and give away the precious little water they had. Surveying all of the 200,000 acres set aside by the Act as Hawaiian Homes Lands, it is clear that most of the lands the Hawaiians were given were among the **worst** lands in the state. And the decent lands given them were in remote, inaccessible areas.

What of the other "boon" for the Hawaiians—the 30% from the sugar lease revenues? With its cap of one million dollars, this was very little money even then to accomplish a terribly big order. It was supposed to pay for roads, water lines, and power lines to distant, inaccessible areas, and it was supposed to pay all the costs of clearing land and building homes, and costs for farm equipment and live stock.

In the sixty-eight years since the Act, even though the million dollar limit for this fund has been lifted twice, less than $14 million has come to the Fund. To pay the huge costs for roads, water, and so forth, the Hawaiian Homes Commission has had to rent out large tracts of the land to non-Hawaiians. About 100,000 acres of Hawaiian Homes Lands are now in the hands of non-Hawaiians—68% of the acreage. And on that acreage, they are getting an average rent of only $16 per acre per year.[42]

In the more than sixty years between 1921 and 1984, only about three thousand applicants received Hawaiian homesteads. That number was doubled in the next four years, although most new applicants who received homesteads are not yet on the land. In 1988 eighteen thousand applicants were still waiting, and two thousand new names were added to the waiting list.[43] Lots that Hawaiians receive today will not bring them back to the land, because the land will not sustain crops. However, with the cost of the average home in Hawaiʻi hovering around $350,000, no matter how desolate and distant the Hawaiian Home Lands may be, they are the only hope many Hawaiians have for ever having a place of their own in their own land.

The new leadership at Hawaiian Homes and a more supportive state government have made great strides in the last few years, but disappointment and frustration were programmed into the Hawaiian Homes Lands project from the beginning. The other half of "the deal," however, was to profit the sugar growers. There was no disappointment or frustration there. The clause in the Organic Act that had limited sugar growers to one thousand acres of lands was deleted.[44] Sugar interests were allowed to renew leases on all of their prime agricultural lands. And sugar lands no longer lay under the threat of possible homesteading. Again the mission boys had come out on top.

One wants to be clear that the Act establishing the Hawaiian Home Lands was never in any way considered a reparations act, compensating Hawaiians for lands taken in the overthrow of the monarchy. The Hawaiian Homes Commission Act was a response to needs of sugar interests.

In the discussions that took place in Congress before passage of the Act, there is a hidden boon for native Hawaiians, however—recognition of their claim to the Ceded Lands. Lawrence Fuchs writes in *Hawai'i Pono*:

> The first resolution passed by the territorial legislature in 1919 requested Congress to set aside certain crown lands—meaning public lands—for the special benefit of the Hawaiian people. A lobbying commission, representing interests friendly to the planters, was appointed to steer the bill through Congress. The commissioners pointed out that in the Great Mahele the commoners did not receive their just share of the lands of the Kingdom. They recalled that with the overthrow of the monarchy, the crown lands, which Kuhio alleged had been set aside as a trust for the common people, were taken over by the Republic, depriving the natives of their rights. On this ground and on the evidence that the Hawaiian race was dying, Kuhio and his supporters justified special treatment for the Hawaiians in the Territory's homestead policies."[45]

A careful study of the discussions in the 1921 Congressional Record regarding the Hawaiian Homes Commission Act establishes that Congress has already recognized the special rights of native Hawaiians to the Ceded Lands, and that it acted in 1921 to establish the Hawaiian Homes Lands because of that recognition. This should serve as a valuable precedent should the Hawaiian people decide to seek "nation within a nation" status with the entire Ceded Lands as their territory.

The Era of the Big Five

It was primarily missionaries and their descendants who got into sugar early. It was the mission boys who formed the core of the all-white Hawaiian League that forced the Bayonet Constitution on King Kalākaua. Again it was they who were the core of the Annexation Club. It was primarily the mission boys who comprised the Committee of Safety. They headed the provisional government and, later, the government of the Republic of Hawai'i. Now, under the Territory, the mission boys who had delivered the islands to the United States prospered beyond their wildest dreams. Their companies became the "Big Five": Castle and Cooke, Alexander and Baldwin, C. Brewer and Co., Theo. Davies & Co., and American Factors. They controlled 75% of the sugar by 1910; by 1933 they controlled 96%. They eventually came to own every business associated with sugar: banking, wholesale and retail merchandising, insurance, utilities, on-island railroad transportation, shipping between the islands, and shipping to and from the continental United States.

Each of the Big Five had a least one direct descendant of a missionary on its board: Alexander, Baldwin, Smith, Castle, Cooke, Judd, Wilcox, Dole, Damon, Thurston, Hall, and Chamberlain—all missionary families—appeared on the boards of almost every important firm that did business in Honolulu. And Walter F. Dillingham, the Big Sixth, was related to the missionary families through his mother. Through interlocking directorates, the missionary families controlled everything that went on in the islands. Their wealth was fabulous.[46]

Adverse Impacts on Native Hawaiians

Native Hawaiians during the time of the Territory were encouraged to "become American," and many did. Any hope of ever having their own nation restored was gone.

Hawaiian language was forbidden in the schools, and many families came to forbid it at home. Passing on the culture was laid aside in many homes.

Hawaiians gave their children American names so that they could fit better into American society. They sent their children to American schools, where they were taught to pledge their allegiance to the United States.

They taught their children to abide by the white man's laws, to adopt his morality, and to try to take on his American lifestyle.

They let their children learn and accept as true the history of Hawai'i from the white man's view.

The radio, the newspaper, everything preached Americanism.

Hawaiian children were taught that their people were lazy, stupid, and worthless, and that they should turn against their culture and make themselves into Yankee adults. With some children it worked. With most, it did not. Many heard they were lazy, stupid, and worthless often enough that they came to believe it.

With the passing of two or three generations under Territorial rule, most Hawaiians not only did not fit in—just as they always had not fit into Western culture—but they had now also surrendered knowledge of their language and their culture.

Worst of all, perhaps, the brainwashing over the decades had convinced most Hawaiians that only a small injustice had been done to their people by the missionaries and their descendants, and by the United States of America.

Statehood

Hawai'i became the 50th State in the Union in 1959. Native Hawaiians again were never asked for their consent. The options available regarding statehood did not allow one to choose between having a Hawaiian nation or having Statehood. One could only choose between having Statehood or continuing the American Territorial Government. It was an American question, asked of Americans: "What kind of Americanism do you choose?" There was no box for checking "None of the above."

In the only two elections where the sentiment of native Hawaiians towards statehood can be gauged--in the Ni'ihau precinct vote and in a straw vote at Kamehameha Schools--the vote was against statehood.

While Statehood has profited almost every group in Hawai'i, it has brought little for the Hawaiian.

Pōkā Laenui (Hayden Burgess) writes of events since Statehood: "We were the target of a free-for-all, "grab whatever you can get" attitude. New economic interests poured into Hawai'i to play the American financial game. Land became the play toy. Selling, trading, leasing, mortgaging, subdividing, became the craze, driving up the price with each change-over. Construction industries changed much of Hawai'i from a lush green paradise, to a cancerous, white, concrete jungle tied together by roadways of asphalt. Foreigners from the United States, Canada, Japan, China, the Arab nations, and elsewhere took "title" to large tracts of land.

"Land today is bartered back and forth with no regard to its spiritual and cultural values or the economic need of the people. Much of it is investor owned, and sits locked up, waiting for price inflation to drive up the speculators' profits. There is minimal concern for the needs of the local people. While empty apartment units are being sold in foreign markets at prices far above our people's abilities to pay, many of our people are sleeping in cars or in parks, hoping to avoid arrest before the morning."[47]

Pōkā Laenui continues, "Any attempt to bring reason to this madness under the American system fails. The people of Hawai'i cannot limit or control this investment madness for several reasons. For one, the present money interests have bought off the pillars of power in Hawai'i. But even if the present State government could be convinced of the ill effects of inter-state and foreign investments in Hawai'i, they could do nothing. For America's foreign investment policies and its federal laws regulating inter-state commerce would pre-empt any laws Hawai'i might enact to solve our problem."[48]

The vote for statehood was also used by the United States to disenfranchise native Hawaiians in another political arena. When the United Nations was formed in 1946, Article 73 of its Charter required nations which had non-self-governing territories to report on the progress of the non-self-governing peoples toward decolonization.

Hawai'i, whose governors were appointed by and answerable to Washington, was a non-self-governing territory and on the list. Like other colonized countries, its rights to decolonization received special protections. In 1960, the U.N. strengthened its support for decolonization by passing Resolution 1514, "The Declaration on the Granting of Independence to Colonial Countries and Peoples." The U.N. also set up a Committee to oversee the application of the Declaration in decolonization efforts. Hawai'i would have been able to apply for assistance from the Committee to help in its decolonization efforts. But in 1959 the United States quietly had Hawai'i removed from the list, using as its justification the vote for Statehood.

Hawaiians justifiably argue that a plebiscite in which more than 90% of the voters were non-native (American military personnel voted too) cannot be used as a vote representing the will of the native people.

Native Hawaiians, who have never voted or agreed in any other way to give away their land, want to again be placed on the U.N. List of Non-Self-Governing Territories and receive U.N. protections in their moves toward decolonization.

The Native Hawaiian Today

TO COMPLETE THE PICTURE of why the native Hawaiian is calling for sovereignty, consider the plight of the Hawaiian today.[1]

Even though there are some Hawaiians who are outstanding scholars, doctors, lawyers, politicians, and businessmen, Hawaiians as a people simply are not making it in modern American society. As a group, they hold the lowest paying jobs in the state. They have the greatest number on welfare. They have the worst housing, if they have housing at all.[2]

Hawaiians rank first with most Western diseases for which records are kept: they have the highest death rate from heart diseases, from stroke, from lung cancer, breast cancer, cancer of the stomach, of the esophagus, of the uterus, and of the pancreas. They have the highest infant mortality rate. And they are first with diabetes, hypertension, and kidney failure.

All of this adds up: the native Hawaiians have the shortest life expectancy of all the peoples in the islands.

There are other areas where Hawaiians aren't making it: they have the highest school drop-out rate. And small as they are in percentage of the state's total population, they far outnumber other nationalities in the jails. In the courts Hawaiians who have held land since the *mahele* have lost thousands of acres to American corporations in "adverse possession" cases. By executive and legislative fiat they have again and again been driven from areas where they have tried to live a traditional, subsistence lifestyle. Modern American society is actually pitted against them.

Where can they turn? Nowhere. Hawaiians rank first in suicide. Their future should lie with their young men. Yet the highest suicide rate in the state is for young Hawaiian men, ages 18-34. There is no place to turn.

As a whole, native Hawaiians clearly are not making it in modern American society. To deny that is to hide one's head in the sand. It is time to deal with this fact squarely, and to find out why.

Those Hawaiians who have "succeeded" are generally from families that have actively sought to become Americanized. Those who have not "succeeded" seem, in various ways, to have resisted Americanization.

One reason those resisting have done so is probably because of a subconscious survival need. The melting pot ideal may be fine for continental America. And it may be fine for foreigners coming to these islands to become Americans. But when Italian Americans or Japanese Americans, for example, lose themselves in American society, there are still Italians and Japanese in the homeland to preserve the national culture. There is no other homeland where Hawaiians are preserving their national culture. This is their only home. As Hawaiians mix in with others, Hawaiian culture, Hawaiian identity, and the Hawaiians as a people, become extinct. Those Hawaiians who resist Americanization know this deep in their being. Their resistance is for survival itself. Hawaiians are a very endangered species living in their one and only habitat.

But there is more to their resistance than this. They resist because they truly **don't fit** in modern Western society. They would not have major problems on every front if they did fit. They are different from Westerners and from Asians, truly different. They are island people whom thousands of years of cultural evolution have formed to interrelate with the land and the sea and other people in a special way in order to assure their survival.

Hawaiians sense differently. They feel the wind differently. They relate to land and sea as family and experience a bond with them which is unknown to Westerners. They have different inner clocks and deal with time differently. They have different priorities in life. They have different strengths. They have different ideas of right and wrong. They get "chicken skin" when they sense a spiritual presence rather than when they feel cold. The list of differences goes on and on. These deep, distinguishing differences are ingrained characteristics selectively acquired and developed over generations for island dwelling.

But while traits such as those mentioned above have prepared Hawaiians excellently for island life, they have also made them extremely vulnerable in modern Western society. Hawaiians need the opportunity and the space to reappropriate, and to revitalize, the culture which they developed over their two-thousand years in these islands. That culture was carefully honed to meet their specific needs, to protect them, to allow them to survive and flourish in their environment, and to give them direction for advancing into the future. Cut off from their culture, they suffer and perish, as they do today.

Their Own Lands—A Survival Need

"**To survive**, the Hawaiian race must have large areas of their ancestral lands returned to them. **To survive,** they must have the space—separate from outsiders—to re-experience the islands and their relationship with them in the same way their ancestors did." "**To survive,**" is a serious claim. On what reasoning is such a claim based?

The question of Hawaiian racial survival may be discussed in the context of evolutionary survival of the fittest. This discussion presumes that evolution is a fact, and that "survival of the fittest" is one of its driving forces. It also presumes that man shares with animals beneath him many of their ways of dealing with reality, among them ways they have developed to achieve the survival of the fittest. Let us examine this further.

Public television in recent years has presented numerous shows on plant and animal life. One of the most interesting topics they have explored has been the mating rituals of animals. One particularly beautiful episode showed two male peacocks prancing before a prospective mate. Male peacocks have beautiful body feathers, but their tail feathers are probably unmatched for beauty in the bird world. The two males fanned out their stunning feathers and strutted around, striking this pose and that pose, and squawking at each other in obvious derision. Eventually, the female chose one over the other and went off with him to mate.

This is what survival of the fittest at its most basic level is all about. Throughout the animal world we find that males and females have arenas of competition to "show their stuff," attempting to prove to prospective partners that they are the best mate for producing the offspring most fit for survival.

This "survival of the fittest" thrust is found at the basis of many human actions and decisions. But since in humans the drive acts primarily on the subconscious level, people are not aware that many of their actions are directed by their need to produce offspring able to adapt to future situations so that the human species will survive.

Humans have many arenas of competition. Often they compete in arenas from which the other sex is entirely excluded. These are fending competitions, practices where they learn their strengths and their weaknesses, sometimes not even realizing that they are competing. But through their activities they slowly establish their position of respect among the peers of their own sex. Those who are superior win the right to be deferred to by those less worthy when beauties of the opposite sex approach. A teenage boy, for instance, may think, "I'm not worthy of her. She will go for him," and leave her for those who have proven themselves better in various areas of competition.

Arenas of competition in the Western world might be the high school football field or basketball court. They might be competitions for the honor roll, for being the drum major or majorette in the band, for the lead in a play, for membership on the debate team, for class president or student body president. Because there are a number of areas in which a species must excel if it is to survive, there are varied arenas for boys or girls with different personalities and different strengths to compete and to prove themselves in order to eventually attract and win the mate whom they choose.

But the arenas of competition in Westerner culture are much different from those in Hawaiian culture. Centuries ago the new belief that nature was "unaware," and incapable of interrelating with man, influenced Western man to distance himself from the world of nature surrounding him. Centuries ago also, the Industrial Revolution took the people who would lead and influence society off the farm and further out of touch with nature. The arenas of competition Westerners slowly devised as proving grounds to demonstrate "fitness" came to be far divorced from nature, and took on radically new and different forms: knowing how to program a computer, to overhaul a car's transmission, and how to correctly punctuate a letter—all signify "the fit." So do having the latest model car and latest fashions in clothes, never being guilty of gaffs in table etiquette, and never wearing a white tie to a black-tie affair. Keeping up with the Joneses is a multi-faceted competition that permeates American society at every level.

Islanders have not shared the changes Europeans and Americans have gone through. In the world view they developed in ancient days, islanders were participants along with the surrounding world of nature in a conscious, interrelating, familial community. As Hawaiian society developed its areas of competition over the centuries, this world view directed selection of the arenas. Hawaiians of old had their "grand arenas" for showing their prowess—the great competititive games of the *Makahiki* celebrations, riddling matches, chant competitions, and *hula* performances, all were grand demonstrations of their physical abilities, their skill or cleverness, or their intellectual acumen. But most of their arenas were closer to the earth and sea, and were much more subtle. The Hawaiian's competition often was a contest with the conscious natural world around him. The firsherman competed with the sea, competed with the fish, with the man-eating shark, and with sudden squalls at sea. Diving down thirty or more feet on a breath of air to lay net or to fish by hand for lobsters in holes on the side of the reef, the Hawaiian was competing, one on one, in a way unknown to continentals. The diver related with the sea, and was at home in the sea. He trusted his gods to protect him, and he depended on his family relationships with the sea and its creatures. If he was family to the sharks, he relied on those related closely to him to protect him. He proved himself every day by coming back alive, or even better, alive and with food in his net. Farmers and other peoples of the land also had their arenas. All the arenas, like the people, were closely tied to nature.

Since the time of Captain Cook, people coming to the islands have transplanted their competitive Western activities here. This has been fine for them, but as the years have passed, and as newcomers have become predominant, they have attempted to impose their culture and their arenas of competition on the Hawaiians. It has not worked.

Instead of realizing that there is nothing at all inside the Hawaiian fisherman, for instance, which would make him in any way whatsoever want to wear a business suit and compete in the stock market, many Westerners seem to insist on just that. One finds an intolerance towards those whose goals do not include living in modern housing, driving new cars, having huge bank accounts, speaking perfect English, and involving themselves in the rush of American society and business. Such a cavalier attitude is found in sentiments such as "Hawaiians would be better off if they took on the American way. This is the modern day, and when Hawaiians catch on and do things our way, they'll be better off."

If people went into the Midwest and made the same proclamations about Midwest farmers, they would be laughed at. No one would consider taking all the people off the farms in the midwest, and changing their lifestyles, their goals, and their realms of competition. Yet many advocate exactly that for the Hawaiians. What is the difference?

Is it that the farmers living "their" different lifestyle perform a service for Americans, and the Hawaiians do not? If that is the case, have Westerners come to the point of facilitating the survival or extinction of a race based on its perceived immediate usefulness?

Certainly it is not desirable to have fewer rather than more distinctive cultures. The greater the variation within a species, the greater the opportunities for further evolution. Variation is the raw material of evolution. The loss of a race—with its physical and mental traits, its philosophy and approach to life, and its traditional lore learned and developed over centuries—is a tragic loss for all mankind. We must preserve the variants. Without them, the future evolution of mankind is limited in its possibilities. For the sake of mankind itself, the Hawaiian race and the Hawaiian culture must be preserved.

To return to our initial topic, arenas of competition are vitally essential for evolutionary advance. Without competition, mankind, at the apex of evolution, cannot choose the best mate, and evolution cannot further progress. Yet it is at this most basic level of existence that Hawaiians are encountering their most fundamental problems.

The Hawaiians' most basic arenas of competition are intertwined with their communal relationship to the land and the sea and the rest of surrounding nature. When Hawaiians were taken from their lands and their traditional ways, when cities were built around them, when their culture was disdained and they were put into Westerners' schools and taught Western values and thought in place of their own—in all these ways Hawaiians were separated from traditional arenas for their competitive "survival of the fittest" rituals. For many, separation from traditional competitions shattered their striving for any goals at all. Today many Hawaiians simply don't compete. The inside drives, for centuries accustomed to work themselves out in certain ways, still surge within. But they are subconscious drives; they are blind by themselves. And the conscious mind is not geared to give them new direction. New arenas have not replaced the traditional ones. Because of this, the Hawaiians' drives to compete and demonstrate fitness and worth are confused, thwarted, and frustrated.

Many young Hawaiians lack goal orientation, lack competition. This is true. But that does not mean these youngsters are lazy. Rather, they do not have a clear view of where they should go, what they should do, what is expected of them. They aren't at home in the Westerner's fields of competition.

In a world where only the fittest survive, every people must have arenas for rituals of competition. If Hawaiians are to have theirs, they must have their lands and seas, and their traditional relationship with them. They must reclaim and revitalize those traditional competitions that evolved over centuries, so that their youth can take them up again, and so that the fittest offspring will emerge. Denied these basic conditions, they cannot survive.

A Note on Resort Developments

It should be noted that the problem of opposing arenas of competition is one aspect of the conflict between Hawaiians and developers. At this writing Hawaiians are protesting three major resort developments in the islands. All three are huge complexes planned for remote parts of the islands. In each case a developer has come in and bought a large section of sea-front land with plans to build a huge resort. People have protested because they don't want their country lifestyle changed. They don't want new people, new houses, more cars, sailboats, motor boats, water skies, jet skies, horses, tourist busses, new stores and tourist traps, and all the support businesses that surround a resort hotel.

The local people do not understand why they should accept a complete change of their life and of the surrounding environment, just because men with no relationship to the land, who are strangers from other areas or from other countries, want to make a fortune for themselves by building an unneeded hotel on a beautiful, uncluttered natural landscape. Also at stake, although not consciously recognized, are the country people's arenas of competition which are inextricably intertwined with their relationship to the sea, the land, and the sky. These arenas of competition are a basic survival need, and Hawaiians can't allow the hotel development without suffering this loss which will ultimately destroy their race. The developer, on the other hand, who subconsciously sees the building of his resort as a personal "proof" that he is among the fittest, does not understand their resistance. He sees forcing his will on others as further proof of his prowess. Rather than deny his manhood by just going away, he goes to court to enforce his will.

It must stop. If it doesn't, there will be no unspoiled beaches and old villages left in the state. Hawai'i is so small. Its distinctive character and lifestyle—its local color—are so fragile. It is being overrun so fast. In another generation, life in Hawai'i will be little different from life in any of southern California's sprawling suburbs. The Hawaiian race, the pure blood, the culture, all will be beyond recapture.

At Cook's arrival there were roughly 1,000,000 pure blooded Hawaiians living in the islands. Today there are a mere 8,244.[3] That is 992,000 less people, a decrease of more than 99%. Today there is not even one pure-blood Hawaiian for every one hundred in pre-Cook times. The Hawaiian race has not just been decimated—it has been almost completely obliterated. Paralleling what has happened to the race, in the years since annexation to America, Hawaiian culture has also been systematically destroyed. Now developers are attacking the last remnants of Hawaiian existence, the country areas of Hawai'i. If there is any hope for Hawaiians to continue "as Hawaiians," it must lie in their ability to reidentify with their roots and to develop a "modern Hawaiianness" on that foundation. With the vestiges of Hawaiian roots found in the quiet, country valleys and seashores that developers are eyeing as "get-away" resorts for wealthy American tourists, and with the American system supporting the entrepreneur and whatever may be his latest scheme to make bucks, what hope is there?

It really must be asked, "Is what is happening to the Hawaiian people America's form of genocide?"

The Need For A Hawaiian Nation

"The solution to the Hawaiians' problems lies in their return to the land and in their reclaiming and developing their traditions and their lifestyle." This thought is not new. It has been expressed over and over again by Hawaiians and non-Hawaiians alike since the time of Kamehameha I.

An Idea Espoused for Two Centuries

When he involved the islands in the sandalwood trade, Kamehameha I ordered his chiefs to send men out to cut trees and to bring them to the ships. So many men were sent from the *ahupua'a* and away from farming that it caused great, and unforeseen, disturbances in society, not the least of which was a famine throughout the islands. "The people were forced to eat herbs and tree ferns, because there was no food to be had."[1] When Kamehameha saw that the country was in the grip of a great famine, he ordered the people "to return to the cultivation of the land." And Kamehameha I himself set the example. Kamakau wrote:

> He himself and those who ate with him (*'ai-alo*) toiled with their own hands to set out a large tract in the uplands of Kailua, known as Kuahewa.[2]

Back to the lands. Back to the traditional ways. That was the solution.

By 1819, the year of Kamehameha's death, many Hawaiians had become convinced that contact with the white man had only brought problems. When his son, Kamehameha II, laid aside the *kapu* system, Kekuaokalani, the great chief who opposed him, clearly saw that this would be the undoing of his people. "Determined to withstand the late innovations and destroy those who introduced and upheld them," Kekuaokalani gathered troops to fight for the restoration of order and the reestablishment of tradition. The majority of the chiefs and the people supported him.[3] Kekuaokalani was killed in battle, however, and with him went the last chance to continue traditional culture uninterrupted.

All was not going well with the adoption of Western ways, however. Threats to expel some or all of the white people continued. Kamehameha II was not happy with the changes in his land. In 1820 he "dispatched his secretary to Honolulu with orders to send out of the country all foreigners who did not hold land. The missionaries were exempted from this order by permission previously given them to remain for a year."[4]

In 1823, the third year after the arrival of the first missionaries, the Reverend William Ellis made a walking journey completely around the Big Island, Hawaii. By this time the diseases of the white man had destroyed three-fourths of the native race, according to Ellis' account. The Reverend sought to convince the people of Waiakea that their own wicked habits and diseases had been the cause of their destruction. He told them that "no remedy [to ward off their total anihilation] was so efficacious as instruction and civilization; and, above all, the principles and doctrines of the bible."[5] And he asked if they would accept a missionary to come and live among them. His journal states,

> Some, however, seemed to doubt the propriety of
> foreigners coming to reside permanently among them.
> They said, they had heard that in several countries, where
> foreigners had intermingled with the original natives, the
> latter had soon disappeared; and, should Missionaries
> come to live at Waiakea, perhaps the land would
> ultimately become theirs, and the *kanaka maore*
> (aborigines) cease to be its occupiers.[6]

Hawaiians thought the means of their own deliverance was in going their traditional way and being left alone by the white man.

Over the next twenty years, the plight of Hawaiians continued to worsen. Many found themselves homeless and hungry in the towns where they were commonly treated as "nigger slaves" by the whites. David Malo and other spokesmen saw return to the lands and traditional ways as the solution to the people's problems. An 1845 petition to the king stated,

> Let the coming of foreigners into this country be delayed
> for ten more years perhaps, and let there be given to us
> lands with the understanding that they are to be
> cultivated....[7]

It was obvious even to the whites in government that Hawaiians were not surviving in the white man's society, and that the answer was a return to the land. *The Polynesian* ran editorials stating that if the Hawaiian people were to be lifted to a higher plane, "the natives need the incentive of individual ownership of home and homestead.... If the native were given a fee simple title to his bit of land, he would then have 'his home, his house, his cattle, the products of his own industry to love, to defend.' He would again become attached to the soil."[8]

Kamehameha III, originally was strongly opposed to the *mahele*—the dividing up of the land and the establishing of private ownership. He finally agreed to it because he saw it as a way to get Hawaiians back on the land. Dr. Gerritt Judd, one of his Privy Councillors, wrote:

> It is the wish of His Majesty, of the Premier, and of the Chiefs, so to improve the tenure and leasing of land as may facilitate its acquisition by the poorer classes, secure a proper reward for their industry, and encourage population by enabling them to provide for and derive profit from their children.[9]

The *mahele* was a monumental failure, however. By 1920, seventy years later, most of the private property in the islands had been bought up by white men. The monarchy, meanwhile, had been overthrown, and the islands had been annexed to the United States.

In 1920, the Congress of the United States was asked to set aside 200,000 acres for native Hawaiian homesteading through the Hawaiian Home Lands Act. "Back to the land! Back to the culture!" was again the solution to the Hawaiian problem argued for in the Congressional debates.   Prince Jonah Kūhiō Kalaniana'ole, Hawai'i's delegate to Congress, and Territorial Senator John Wise testified that the purpose of the rehabilitation measure "was to save the Hawaiian people from extinction by returning them to the land." [The Act would] "give them the mode of living that their ancestors were accustomed to, and in that way rehabilitate them."[10]

The Hawaiian Home Lands were established, but the "Back to the land, back to culture" intent was thwarted by the fact that most of the lands were of such poor quality they defied cultivation.

The two-hundred-year-long conviction that Hawaiian survival depends on "return" is still strong today. It has been seen in the "Keep the Country Country" protests on the Windward Coast of O'ahu in the 1970s; in the standoff at Sand Island on O'ahu where Hawaiians living their traditional way were labeled "squatters," were carried away by force, and had their fishing village levelled; in the resistance of the people to being moved off of the seashores at Mākua and at Waimānalo Beach in the early 1980s, and in other protest actions. All of these are present day restatements of what Hawaiians have been saying from the time of Kamehameha I: "So many Hawaiians are not surviving in the world of the white man. Give us our lands and seas, and let us return to the ways of our culture. Hawaiians can survive if they can be Hawaiian and live Hawaiian."

Some Questions, Some Answers

Question: "So Hawaiians and others have consistently argued for two centuries that the solution to the Hawaiians' problems is having lands of their own and having the opportunity to reclaim and revitalize their culture. What reason is there to think that if they are given lands, they will attempt to reappropriate their culture? Handing over the state, or even half of the it, is a pretty big step to make without any assurance of success."

Answer: No absolute guarantees can be given, of course. But if one looks at the inner dynamics of Hawaiian groups that have grown up in the last two decades, whether they be *hālau* for teaching *hula*, the Polynesian Voyaging Society, new Hawaiian Civic Clubs, protest groups, or pro-sovereignty groups, one finds as a central concern the study and practice of aspects of Hawaiian culture. The entire Hawaiian renaissance of the '70s and '80s is itself a demonstration of broad and sincere interest in reappropriating Hawaiian tradition and living it in modern times.

Question: "If Hawaiians are given lands, and if they should reappropriate and revitalize their culture, what reasons are there to think that this will solve their problems?"

Answer: Many indicators suggest that return to the land will be the solution. Great numbers of Hawaiians who are forced to live according to white customs and compete in the white world are not making it. Yet, in rural areas where Hawaiians farm, fish, and practice their culture, they are happy, fulfilled, and flourishing.

The idea that "return" is the solution also can certainly claim the wisdom of ages. Both kings and commoners have consistently advocated it for two hundred years.

And while success cannot be guaranteed, simple justice demands that it be tried. The Hawaiians have been illegally and immorally dispossessed of their homeland by the American nation. President Grover Cleveland stated this unequivocally in a formal message to the Congress. Justice demands the return of Hawaiian lands, and the opportunity for Hawaiians to revive their culture and survive as a people.

Question: "When speaking of "lands where Hawaiians can reappropriate their culture," is some kind of separation of Hawaiians from non-Hawaiians envisioned? And, if so, why?

Answer: The Maori, the Polynesians of New Zealand, have the space to practice their traditional ways, alone and away from others. They have been able to hold on to large areas of their original lands. Their *marae*—their traditional village meeting halls and ceremonial grounds—are still vibrant centers of native life, where the cultural heritage is kept intact and passed on.

In Western Samoa, and in many other island groups of Polynesia, little of the original culture is changed. People live in the way that centuries of experience have taught them is best for island people. In much of Polynesia, foreigners cannot buy land: culture is preserved through separation from outsiders.

Many American Indian tribes similarly have been able to preserve and perpetuate their culture because of separation—the distance from others—afforded them by having their own lands.

If Hawaiians are to succeed in rebuilding their culture, they also need buffer zones to separate themselves from Western society. Hawaiians need areas where they can **be Hawaiian,** where they can live together in the Hawaiian way and let their culture evolve naturally.

Question: "Is it expected that Hawaiians will **all** return to an ancient lifestyle?"

Answer: This is certainly an important question. It is certainly not expected that there will be a mass return to the ancient lifestyle.

Perhaps only a small number will return to living in the old ways when given the opportunity. But when they do, they will need valleys, mountains, and seas where they can pursue the ancient lifestyle freely. Such settlements will become centers for Hawaiian culture, and may serve as retreats to which others can come to live temporarily and to learn through experience the traditional culture of their people.

Most likely the majority of Hawaiians will prefer to continue the lifestyle lived by so many in the Hawaiian homestead areas today: a country, subsistence lifestyle amid more modern conveniences. For this they will need rural lands where they can live close to the earth and close to the sea. Some will need good agricultural lands where crops will grow, and access to fresh water for their farming. Others will need quiet, uncluttered seas they can fish.

And certainly, many other Hawaiians will also want to continue living "the American way." Those who wish to fully embrace the modern American lifestyle, yet to do so while living among their own people and receiving the support of their culture, will also need homes in the Hawaiian lands.

One should not envision great masses of Hawaiians moving out of the towns and cities and off to "Hawaiian areas." Initially, at least, most Hawaiians probably would not move from their present neighborhoods. Many Hawaiians are perfectly happy living the Western way in neighborhoods that are almost completely non-Hawaiian. Further, many Hawaiians probably already live in areas that would become part of the nation. The homesteads, for example, would be part of the Hawaiian nation.

Question: "Would 'reappropriating traditional culture' involve a return to the ancient world-view described in *A Hawaiian Nation I Man, Gods, and Nature?*"

Answer: That would be most desirable. The traditional Hawaiian view is a viable way of approaching reality even today. It is a fascinating alternative world view, different from any found outside of Polynesia. It is worthy of development. And certainly it is true that every additional school of lived philosophy that the world can preserve enhances mankind's chances of discovering, and making, the best evolutionary choices to preserve and develop the human race.

If the Hawaiian world view is going to serve people today, it will need development. It will need modernization, application to present day situations. It might be helpful to discuss how another people went about a similar modernization.

Reclaiming and Modernizing Tradition

One of history's greatest and most successful social experiments began in circumstances somewhat similar to those of present day Hawaiians. It was a social change that served the Chinese people well, allowing them to advance and prosper for two thousand years. It began with Confucius who lived five hundred years before Christ. Confucius was a lover of the ancients. From his youth, he immersed himself in the ancient classics, works which by then were a thousand years old. He practiced ancient arts and sports, and imbued himself with the ancient thought-framework and traditional values. Confucius lived at a time of great disruption in China: the Chou dynasty, which had existed for seven hundred years was in its final

stages of collapse. China was sliding into the horror of the
Warring States period when rival baronies would ravage
and plunder one another, sometimes beheading all the
citizens in a newly conquered territory. In the anarchy of
the four-hundred years surrounding the life of Confucius,
the traditional way of life, and the *mores* and customs which
governed and guided society, were abandoned and
eventually forgotten. Identity with the past was lost.

Finally, needing to bring the chaos and anarchy to an end,
people searched for some way to pull their society together
again. What they found and rallied around were the
teachings of Confucius.

The traditions of peoples emerge unconsciously out of
trial and error over innumerable generations. Tradition
holds the wisdom of the ages; it embodies what works for a
people. But as Confucius realized, tradition is also dynamic:
it can and should be modernized and adapted to
present-day situations. He did that. Keeping the ancient
Classics as his sole source, he modified, reinterpreted, and
updated them. While preserving the ties with the past,
Confucius taught his followers the thought of the ancients as
intelligently applied to modern times.

When the centuries of the Warring States period was
coming to an end, and the Chinese were looking for ways to
pull their society together and live together again, the school
of Confucius was there offering to reacquaint them with
their traditional culture and values. Like Hawaiians today,
who continue to do things in "Hawaiian ways" even though
the reasons for doing things those ways are lost, the Chinese
similarly had retained traces of traditional ways in their
lifestyle. Because those traces were there, they found

Confucianism to resonate with their innermost being. In it they could see and identify with their roots. Confucianism was "them!"

The Chinese adopted Confucianism and made it the center of their societal renewal. They established Confucianist schools throughout the land, and taught both the ancient classics and their modern applications to a people who had long forgotten their culture. Through Confucian schools they moved "doing things the Chinese way" from the unconscious level to the conscious level. They painstakingly formed a new culture which, though modern, was was truly traditional "Chinese." And for two thousand years, that culture has guided and protected them and allowed them to flourish.[11]

Like the Chinese, the Hawaiians will have to modernize their ancient traditions and then consciously form a new culture, a new society. Firmly based in their cultural heritage, the modernized culture will be truly Hawaiian.

Other Possible Developments
That Might Be Anticipated

As noted above, no great exodus of Hawaiians from their present homes in cities and towns to new homes in the territory of the Hawaiian Nation is anticipated. One can, however, expect a decided turn toward the study and readoption of traditional ways among those who choose to move to the lands of the new Hawaiian nation and among those living on the homesteads. Let us discuss some other developments that may be anticipated.

When Hawaiians live among Hawaiians, they will increase their opportunities to meet and marry a person of their own race. Today there are barely eight thousand pure-blood Hawaiians.[12] Yet pure-blood and mixed-blood Hawaiians continue at an alarming rate to further dissipate their descendants' percentage of Hawaiian ancestry through intermarriage. Proportionally, Hawaiians exceed every other people on earth in entering interracial marriages. Although, it is commonly accepted that further dilution of Hawaiian blood by mixed marriages must be ebbed, there seems no way to stop it. Incentives to marry Hawaiian will not help; Hawaiians marry for love. The only hope is to surround young people with enough of their own race that they will meet and fall in love with another Hawaiian.

Once on their own lands, Hawaiians will need their own leaders: their own *ali'i nui* (ruler) and other *ali'i*—chosen by whatever method they decide upon, election or heredity. Hopefully, these *ali'i* will reestablish their special chiefly relationship with the lands. Hopefully, they will guide the people in readopting the traditional view that humans participate with surrounding nature in a consciously interrelating, familial, world community in which all care for and protect one another.

The people will need to recontact and reaffirm their ties with the living and conscious cosmos about them. They will need to reclaim their spiritual heritage, to develop that spiritual awareness which for centuries so characterized the race. They will need to reconfirm their own societal values and morals. And they will need the opportunity to nourish their relationship with their ancestral spirits, and to publicly worship their ancient gods if that is their choice.

Hawaiians will need a system of laws suited to their culture.

Traditional roles and occupations will also need to be resurrected and reinstated. Practicing traditional roles gives one character, refinement, and fulfillment. Hawaiian society had a place for farmers, fishermen, and keepers of fishponds, for artists and craftsmen, dancers and chanters, wrestlers, spearmen and warriors, tattooers and composers, teachers, navigators, prophets and healers, priests, and chiefly leaders—to name just a few of the roles for men. If Hawaiian culture were earnestly being perpetuated in Hawaiian communities, Hawaiian men and women could make a living and win honor and respect while pursuing traditional occupations.

Hawaiians had a traditional diet which made them strong, huge, and healthy, and at the same time lithe, agile, and beautiful. Recent studies with Hawaiians who have readopted the traditional diet show a dramatic drop in high blood cholesterol—a major risk factor in heart attacks now so prevalent among Hawaiians. It is thought that a return to the traditional diet will bring a marked decrease in many types of disease. Today traditional Hawaiian foods are too expensive for even most middle-income families in Hawai'i to afford on a regular basis. If the people can get back to the good lands and begin growing their own crops, supply should meet the demand, and prices will come down to where the healthy Hawaiian diet will be within the economic reach of all Hawaiians.

Hawaiians need the opportunity to readopt their native language. There has been strong non-Hawaiian resistance, even recently, to the use of Hawaiian language in the schools. In 1987, the State Department of Education finally allowed Hawaiian language experts to begin two experimental Hawaiian-language immersion programs. In two different schools first-grade classes were taught for a year using only the Hawaiian language. End of year tests showed that children in the two Hawaiian immersion classes, besides doing very well in all other subjects, also **tested higher in English** than other first graders in the state whose classes were entirely taught in English.[13] The program was equally successful when expanded to follow the children into higher grades. These programs are continuing to expand, as they must. Hawaiian and English are both official languages of the State of Hawai'i.

With or without the prospect of nationhood, public schools with large percentages of Hawaiian students need a thorough overhauling. The situation for native Hawaiian children in elementary schools is, at best, unacceptable. The situation for native Hawaiians in high school is deplorable. The schools that score lowest in the state are schools in which the Hawaiian population is highest.[14] A basic problem is that the "American" education presented is not culturally relevant for Hawaiians. American education is founded in American culture; it finds its references in that culture. School children in continental America learn well because what they are taught in their classes and what they read in their books has reference to and is supported by the world they experience. Schools in Hawai'i take the same books and same lessons which relate to the continental American culture and experience, and attempt to teach the native islanders through them, foreign as the material might be to everything native children experience. This has not worked in the past; it does not work now; and it will not work in the future. For Hawaiian children, the world referred to in American text books is an abstraction. One must be able to deal with abstractions to handle an abstract world. While the most brilliant native children can handle abstract concepts and can profit from this kind of education, the ordinary child cannot, for the average child of any race has trouble with abstraction. American education goes over the Hawaiian child's head. He gets bored because he doesn't understand the references. He begins to see that school is a waste of his time: he doesn't know what is going on, and he "isn't learning anything." It is only a matter of time before he drops out. Dropouts, however, go through life thinking of themselves as failures looked down upon by society. With such low self esteem—caused by the school system itself—it is a wonder if he is a success at anything.

Why are native Hawaiian children given books about Dick and Jane and Spot? Why are they given books about life in the ghetto or the barrio? Fantastic stories to which they can relate abound in their own tradition. Why can they not learn those stories in school? Why can they not learn biology by learning Hawaiian plants and animals? Why can't their interest in geography be piqued by teaching them the locations and circumstances surrounding places famous in Hawaiian lore first, then moving out into the Pacific from which they came, and only then tackling the geography of the rest of the world? Why can't math be taught while constructing a canoe or building a house? What good is Spanish going to do them, and why is it pushed on them in preference to the Hawaiian language? Why do Hawaiian students spend a year learning the history of America? And why, when they are old enough to think for themselves—in the eleventh grade—are they only taught "modern" Hawaiian history which begins with Annexation and tells the glories of the white man's achievements? Where is the history of the Hawaiian people? Where are the stories of their own great heros? Homemaking classes teach American homemaking, customs, and values. Cooking classes neglect to teach traditional preparation of traditional Hawaiian foods. The Department of Education is so caught up in the great American-melting-pot ideal, that it is neglecting its duty to make classes culturally relevant enough to educate the children native to these islands.

Hawaiian youth must be rescued from the present day schools of the State.

Or the schools must change. Cultural practice and traditional knowledge must be passed on if the culture is to survive. The school is the most viable structure we currently have for doing this.

If Hawaiian children had their lessons taught from within their cultural framework, they too would learn their culture while learning reading, math, history, geography, biology, homemaking and so forth. Given the amount of television students watch today, there can be little fear that in getting rid of continental American textbooks, Hawaiian children will not learn enough about America.

Hawaiians need schools that will immerse their children in their cultural heritage and their language, that will teach them their stories and myths and cultural practices, that will embue them with their ancient world-view and values, that will train them in their ancient skills, that will employ their innate memory and chant abilities, and develop their musical and poetic talent. They need schools where children will learn their strengths and be spurred on to excellence through traditional Hawaiian competition, schools that will excite them about life and fill them with happiness and pride—that will give them support in their innermost "island-child" beings. They need curricula which will educate Hawaiian children from within their own cultural context, yet at the same time will prepare them well to meet with success in the modern Western world.

Both within and without college or university walls, the Hawaiian intellectual tradition itself also must be further developed and made available to the rest of the world. Because the Hawaiians were island people and had to look at the world differently, they developed explanations far different from others for how the cosmos and all of the things in it work and how they interrelate with one another. In the present intellectual climate, with scholars increasingly looking beyond Western thought to alternative insights and solutions devised by other peoples, the Hawaiian intellectual tradition has much to offer in the areas of psychology and psychiatry, philosophy, religion, biology, astronomy, and environmental studies.

Hawaiians must have the freedom to develop as Hawaiians—to take their two-thousand-year-old culture and let it become all that it can become over the next two thousand years.

Summary

Before moving on to discuss the history of the sovereignty movement, let us take a moment to reflect on all that has been read so far, and relate it to why Hawaiians must insist on a change in their relationship with the United States.The Hawaiian call for sovereignty is based on three facts: 1) that the actions which have dispossessed them from their lands and their lawful government and have brought them under the control of America were all contrary to international law or American constitutional law at the time they took place; 2) that America has not fulfilled its obligation to care for and protect the Hawaiian people, an obligation that must be expected of a legitimate government; and 3) that Hawaiians have an inherent right to continue to exist as a distinct people of the earth, and, therefore, given both the decimation of their race and their culture that has taken place, Hawaiians must pursue some other political relationship with the United States in order to survive as a people.

The Sovereignty Movement—
Where It Came From And Where It Is Today

The Beginning of the Sovereignty Movement

After decades that saw Hawaiians denying and neglecting their cultural heritage, the early 1970s brought a renewal of interest in traditional Hawaiian music, arts, and crafts. A book by John Dominis Holt, *On Being Hawaiian*, is often credited with sparking the Hawaiian renaissance. A bold statement for its time, it refuted many false claims commonly passed on about Hawaiians and Hawaiian culture, it noted a number of great achievements of the Hawaiian people throughout history, and it proclaimed the author's pride in being Hawaiian. The time was right. Tourism had grown and thousands of people were arriving in the islands hoping to see something truly Hawaiian. It was okay to be Hawaiian again. The renaissance quickly grew into a wide-ranging renewal of interest that continues today. College courses began to be offered exploring ancient knowlege and practice. And Hawaiians began to be **proud** of being Hawaiian again.

As interest in their roots grew, Hawaiians came to study their genealogies and family traditions. As they went into their family histories, many discovered that thousands of acres had been taken from their families by the courts through the years, using the law of adverse possession. They began to piece together how the white man's laws in the white man's courts had been used to dispossess and impoverish their families. And they began to look further. They knew their kingdom had been overthrown by the white man, and that the white man could not justify that act—although post-monarchy history books did not share that view. Hawaiians began to study history with an eye to finding illegal actions taken in the overthrow of 1893 which might be used as a basis for legal claims for reparations. Researchers were unprepared for what they found. They had been educated to think of America as righteous. To deny the righteousness of America was like denying the goodness of a part of themselves. But there in historical documents were clear statements of America's complicity in a conspiracy to overthrow the Hawaiian kingdom. Who would believe them? Who even among their own people?

Events taking place, however, would cause the people to believe. The growth of tourism was accompanied by a growth in new residents coming to the islands. The eastern part of the island of O'ahu was being developed with expensive homes for newcomers. As the housing stretched farther, Henry J. Kaiser announced his intention to build high-priced homes in Kalama Valley. To do this, pig farmers, and many other Hawaiian and non-Hawaiian families had to be evicted. Not only would lives be disrupted, but a "way of life" for local people would be destroyed to make way for rich newcomers. People banded together to protest the development. They formed an organization, Kōkua Kalama, and engaged in demonstrations. A number were arrested on trespassing charges. Eventually the local people were evicted and the expensive houses built. But the Kalama Valley protest of 1970 had played an important role in the development of social activism and self-determination among Hawaiians. It caused people to begin questioning and investigating the actions of big business and government. And for the first time in decades, it had brought Hawaiians to action.[1]

Over the next few years more groups were organized to stand up for Hawaiian rights. The first to focus on reparations for the overthrow of the monarchy was A.L.O.H.A. —Aboriginal Lands of Hawaiian Ancestry— founded in 1972, by Louisa K. Rice. Two factors influenced Mrs. Rice. After reading the autobiography of Queen Lili'uokalani, *Hawaii's Story by Hawaii's Queen*, she was deeply moved by the injustice done to the Hawaiian people in the take-over of their nation.[2] And the Alaska Native Claims Settlement Act of 1971 had just been passed. Through that Act "the United States returned 40 million acres of land to the Alaskan natives and paid $1 billion cash for land titles they did not return."[3] Mrs. Rice thought the United States should treat the Hawaiians similarly. She first organized A.L.O.H.A. with her family members, and then expanded to include other people on Moloka'i. One and a half years later, there were 9000 members across the state. To date, 30,000 people have paid their $1 membership dues.[4]

In 1973, A.L.O.H.A. raised $150,000 through a twenty-hour telethon broadcast from 'Iolani Palace. This did much to publicize and gain popular support for the A.L.O.H.A. issues and claims.[5] Former Congressman and Secretary of the Interior, Stewart Udall, was hired to draw up a bill for reparations to present to the Congress. Udall had previously worked with the Alaskan natives in successfully securing their reparations.

The Hawaiian delegation to Congress entered the bill in 1974. It "demanded a cash payment to the Hawaiian people for losses of lands, resources, rights, and revenues sustained as a result of the overthrow and subsequent annexation by the United States."[6] Several hearings were held and, for a few years, the bill was reintroduced in one form or another, but no effective legislative action was taken.[7]

Congress eventually set up a Study Commission to make a recommendation. The majority of the people appointed to the "Native Hawaiians Study Commission" of 1983 were mid-level Washington bureaucrats, who admittedly knew little or nothing about Hawai'i. They were given only **six** months of actual working time. There was too much for them to read, absorb, and analyze within that time. The members from Washington also seemed to lack the necessary skills and training required for the job they were mandated to do. As the Hawaiian members wrote in their dissenting opinion, "their findings, conclusions, and recommendations derived from flawed methodology, limited research, and too-restrictive applications of inappropriate legal analysis."[8]

As an example of limited research, in most cases researchers presenting material for study by the commission were not directed to use original sources. Much of the time, the only source used was the three volume history, *The Hawaiian Kingdom*, by Ralph S. Kuykendall. Kuykendall had been invited to Hawai'i in 1922 by the territorial government to write the textbook on Hawaiian history that would be used in the schools. The textbook was to tell the American view of Hawaiian history to children who were now Americans.[9] Kuykendall was expected to present facts that would make the government then in power look noble and just—the rescuers of Hawai'i from the monarchy.

His later three volume work, *The Hawaiian Kingdom,* which was used so often as a source by the Native Hawaiians Study Commission, is written in a style that suggests dispassionate objectivity. But it presents Hawaiian history from a pro-American prejudice that is not immediately apparent to Americans: it tells Hawai'i's story by relating selected facts which reflect the American value system, and American ideals and goals. And it arranges these facts in a sequence historically developing America's fulfillment of its "manifest destiny" in the Pacific.[10]

Relying on Kuykendall and other American writers with similar "American" perspectives, the majority of the Native Hawaiian Study Commission was subject to an inadequate and prejudiced view of events.

But that wasn't the worst of it: in an astonishing move that outraged many knowledgeable observers, the commission enlisted the historians of the U.S. Navy to prepare the most sensitive area of their research.[11] Observers were incensed because they believed that the U.S. Navy—in its desire for permanent control of Pearl Harbor—was the instigator behind the American moves leading up to and bringing about the overthrow of the monarchy. Now the Navy itself was actually in control of what material would be seen in the investigation. The Navy files perhaps would have been the best place to find incriminating evidence, but the Navy was not parting with any of it. The Study Commission could have demanded files, but the Navy historians were asked only for a review of secondary sources. Not about to offer what wasn't requested, researchers at the Naval Historical Center sent a short review that basically quoted Kuykendall, Tate, and the Blount Report.[12]

The majority report submitted by the Study Commission in 1983 recommended against reparations to the native Hawaiian people for the American overthrow of their government.

As Senator Daniel Inouye has stated, "As soon as the commission report was released, it was severely criticized by scholars, lawyers and, of course, Hawaiian leaders. The criticism focused on the dubious findings of fact related to the historical role of the United States. Particularly compelling was the testimony of the Library of Congress on the procedures employed by the commission."[13]

Chairperson Kina'u Boyd Kamali'i and others on the Study Commission who disagreed with the majority filed a minority report which strongly supported reparations, but it was ignored by the Congress.[14] Five more years would pass before any further Congressional action.

But we have jumped way ahead of our story. Return to the early '70s. Protests mounted on various islands over encroachments on Hawaiian country living and over evictions to make way for large scale development. In 1971 residents of Halawa Housing contested their eviction by the state. They lost. In 1974 the Waiāhole-Waikāne Community Association, made up of farmers, tenants, and small landowners, challenged their eviction by the McCandless heirs to make way for development. This time the state purchased Waiāhole Valley and negotiated leases for the people. In 1975 fishermen on Mokauea Island organized to protest their eviction from the island and were successful in negotiating a sixty-year low rent lease to construct a new fishing village.[15] Although not directly focused on sovereignty, these protests had overtones and undertones of native Hawaiian self-determination.

Groups specifically dedicated to Hawaiian sovereignty also arose. In 1974, 'Ohana O Hawai'i (The Extensive Family of Hawai'i) was founded. Their political and spiritual leader, Peggy Ha'o Ross, while living in Oregon, twice had experiences of being confronted with a bright light and in those encounters receiving a message to come home. When she eventually did return to Hawai'i, it became clear to Mrs. Ross that while Queen Lili'uokalani had agreed to no longer lay claim to her throne, the Hawaiian **people** had never surrendered their sovereignty. The Hawaiian people were still sovereign. There was only an "empty throne." Peggie Ha'o Ross organized her relatives and followers into a Hawaiian nation, and she assumed the throne for the time being, as the sovereign leader of the Hawaiian nation. Over the years 'Ohana O Hawai'i has made many contributions. They have taken the case of the illegally overthrown Hawaiian nation before the World Court at The Hague, and before a number of other international tribunals, calling for the decolonization of Hawai'i, and laying the groundwork for recognition of an eventual declaration of actual sovereignty. 'Ohana O Hawai'i is now perhaps the largest in numbers of the present-day sovereignty groups.[16]

Another pro-sovereignty organization founded in this period was the Protect Kaho'olawe 'Ohana (P.K.O.). In 1975, members of A.L.O.H.A. and another group, Hui Ala Loa, grew tired of waiting for Congress to take action on the reparations bills. They organized a symbolic landing on the sacred island of Kaho'olawe, which the military had taken over for bombing practice during World War II. Out of this action grew the Protect Kaho'olawe 'Ohana ('*Ohana* here means "extensive family") led by George Helm and Walter Ritte. Hawaiians outside of the P.K.O. initially were horrified at their own people so brazenly taking on the American military. Protests against the state over evictions were one thing, but now activists were taking on the federal government which Hawaiians at all societal levels had grown up thinking of as good, benevolent and protective. P.K.O. members continued making allegedly illegal protest landings on the island, however. And under the leadership of Walter Ritte and the medical doctor, Emmett Aluli, they took their case to court. They have been amazingly successful. They have won the clean-up of the island and its return from the military. A conveyance committee is deciding if it is possible to convey the island directly to native Hawaiians.[17]

As the P.K.O. was waging its battles, other protests were going on. In 1979, calling them squatters, the state evicted Hawaiians from their fishing village at Sand Island on O'ahu. Hawaiians living the hand-to-mouth subsistence lifestyle of traditional fishermen, were now being forced from their homes, their livelihood, and their native lifestyle. The nightly television news covered their forceful eviction and the subsequent levelling of their homes and won them much popular support.

These confrontations all added to Hawaiians' awareness that they could fight back. They served as building blocks in the growing Hawaiian support for self-determination and sovereignty. However, large numbers of Hawaiians still looked upon the protests with disdain and viewed them as shameful.

This view largely changed with the "beach people" incidents. In the 1970s the speculative craze in real estate had gone berserk. Homes priced at $10,000 in the 1960s had skyrocketed to $120,000 by 1980; rents had jumped from $100 to $600 a month (cheap as that may seem now). Hawaiians at the bottom of the economic ladder could not pay for shelter. They were forced to live in cars and on the beaches. This went on for more than a year and was a steadily growing problem.

The state initially looked upon the destitute "beach people" as a blight hurting the tourist industry. Tourists couldn't get to the beaches easily, and the closely crowded tents were an eyesore that made wealthy travellers feel uncomfortable. The "beach people" were giving the state a bad name. They had to go. But where? Initially they were given land on which there was no water. It was a situation worse than the seashores, and the people resisted. When the State began to evict them from the beaches of Mākua, Nānākuli, Waimānalo, and Makapu'u, the evening news carried heart-wrenching scenes of police carrying handcuffed fathers and mothers off to jail while their young children, screaming hysterically, were held back by other police. The "beach people" were primarily Hawaiians, evicted from the last place available to them in their own land. This outrageous treatment of their fellow Hawaiians did much to solidify the majority of the native people in support of the protests.

There were other demonstrations—at Nukoli'i on Kaua'i in 1982,[18] at Mākena on Maui in 1984,[19] at West Beach on

O'ahu[20] in 1986—against luxury resorts and housing developments which would bring thousands of tourists and workers into sometimes quite remote areas and would change the traditional lifestyles of the people. Still other battles were fought, such as that of the Hawaiian leprosy patients fighting to prevent relocation to another hospital from Hale Mohalu, the hospital home they had known most of their lives.[21] Efforts also were made to prevent desecration of the volcano goddess, Pele, by drilling geo-thermal wells into the Kīlauea volcano.[22] At South Point on the Big Island Hawaiians protested the taking of Hawaiian Home Lands to build a Spaceport.[23] Others have protested the moving of Hawaiian graves to make way for a hotel on the island of Maui.[24] All these demonstrations have had overtones of Hawaiian sovereignty and have pointed to the need for greater organization in order to reclaim what is rightfully the Hawaiians'.

More sovereignty groups have formed. Mililani Trask, a Hawaiian lawyer, sent out a statewide call for a Constitutional Convention for a Hawaiian Nation. In early 1987, delegates from every island attended the first session and drafted a tentative Constitution. It has four branches of government, adding to the executive, legislative, and judicial a position for an *ali'i nui* (high chief) and his/her advisory council. Mililani Trask was elected to a four year term as Kia'āina, (president or head of the Executive branch). Delegates of Ka Lāhui Hawai'i (literally "The Hawaiian Nation"), have met in Convention a number of times since. In 1989, as planned, they held a second Constitutional Convention to revise that document, having lived with it for two years. Native Hawaiian membership in Ka Lāhui Hawai'i numbers more than 8,000 at this writing.[25]

Nā 'Ōiwi o Hawai'i (The Native Hawaiians), another group, with its leaders, Soli Niheu and 'Imaikalani Kalāhele has sponsored a number of rallies calling for restoration which have been well-covered by the press. In 1985 they sponsored "Ho'okū'oko'a 1985," a forum on Nationalism and Independence at the Kamehameha Schools.[26]

Individual Hawaiian spokespersons such as Professor Haunani-Kay Trask of the Center for Hawaiian Studies at the University of Hawai'i have drawn attention to the issue through speeches, writings, and participation in demonstrations. Attorney Pōkā Laenui (Hayden Burgess) has become involved in international organizations such as the World Council of Indigenous Peoples, and the International Work Group for Indigenous Affairs, and has taken the cause of the Hawaiian people before the International Labor Organization in Geneva and other international tribunals. La France Kapaka has moved ahead as if the nation were already reestablished: she has involved more than 300 Hawaiians in traditional Hawaiian farming in Hanalei Valley on Kaua'i, living off the land while re-learning Hawaiian culture. Louis Agard and John Agard of the Council of Hawaiian Organizations, Japanese lawyer Mitsuo Uyehara, scholar-activist Professor Marion Kelly, John Kelly with his basement print shop, *kumu* Thomas Maunupau, composer Liko Martin, and respected community leader Genesis Lee Loy are just a few of the many individuals who through the years have been eloquent advocates and tireless workers for sovereignty.

The Office of Hawaiian Affairs must also be recognized as solidly committed to the return of land and self-government for the Hawaiian people. Established at the 1978 Constitutional Convention for the State of Hawai'i, the

Office of Hawaiian Affairs was organized to receive and to spend for the benefit native Hawaiians a portion of the income from leases of the Ceded Lands. OHA, as it is called, is also charged with holding the State accountable for its administration of both the Hawaiian Home Lands and the Ceded Lands. Frenchy De Soto, Rod Burgess, Clarence F.T. Ching, Moanikeala Akaka, Clayton Hee, and the other OHA trustees have broadened the scope of the Office to include advocating for self-government.[27]

The trustees of OHA, elected statewide, say that OHA has the established organization to begin acting as the ruling body of the Hawaiian nation, should it be given the lands, the money, and recognition as the government. However, OHA, as presently constituted and empowered, is an agency of the State of Hawai'i, established by its Constitution, and funded by its legislature. It is far too subject to control by the State to be entrusted with the sovereignty of the Hawaiian people. As trustee Clarence Ching has acknowledged, if the Office of Hawaiian Affairs were to enter itself as a candidate for governing, it would have to reconstitute itself as completely distinct from the State and totally sovereign.[28] Otherwise, another organization such as one of those mentioned above must be selected to govern.

The American Indians

Before going further with this thumbnail history of the Hawaiian sovereignty movement, it will be helpful to insert some background on developments between the American Indians and the federal government. In 1954, although most Americans were unaware of it, the federal government, through Congress, adopted a policy of termination of tribal governments. This policy which was in effect until 1970, forced many tribes to terminate their status as nations and to surrender their federal benefits—in a word, to detribalize. Many tribes felt powerless and went along, allowing their lands to be sold, taking one-time cash payments against claims, dissolving their tribal membership, and allowing their people to be repatriated as individual citizens of only the United States of America.

Seeing the success that the Civil Rights movement was having, however, Indians of many tribes came to realize that they too could fight against what was wrong. Indians began to educate themselves and to study the political process. Young people became attorneys. They studied Indian tribal laws, and they learned about the legal rights of native people in American law. They learned how to challenge the federal government and to use American law to protect and advance themselves. Once they had their act together, they took their cases to the courts, legislatures, and Congress. They have had phenomenal success. In some cases tribes have retribalized with far more than they had when they were forced to detribalize.

There are over five hundred American Indian attorneys today. Cases they have fought and won have established a strong body of legal precedents and opinions upon which Hawaiians, as native Americans, can also draw.

The Indians eventually formed the Native American Rights Fund to pool their knowledge and resources. In 1986 the Native American Rights Fund (NARF) voted to become officially active in native Hawaiian rights issues. In 1987 they elected the first native Hawaiian to their Board of Directors, sealing their commitment to the Hawaiian people. Currently, they are actively working with lawyers of the

Native Hawaiian Legal Corporation, their Hawaiian counterpart, laying the legal groundwork for the sovereignty case.[29]

The Native Hawaiian Rights Meeting

Returning to the history of the Hawaiian sovereignty movement, on August 5-7 of 1988 a large number of individuals and representatives from several of the sovereignty groups came together at a Native Hawaiian Rights Conference sponsored by the Office of Hawaiian Affairs and the Native Hawaiian Legal Corporation. The conference was held at the Kamehameha Schools. An early speaker at the conference was Charles F. Wilkinson, an attorney for the Native American Rights Fund (NARF) who is also a professor of law at the University of Colorado. Wilkinson had joined NARF in 1971, had successfully represented tribes in court, before legislatures, and in Congress, and had recently published a book on the Supreme Court's development of Indian law over the past twenty-five years.[30]

Many points from Wilkinson's talk are relevant to this discussion. He initially addressed the feeling shared by many in the movement at that time that they were doing something wrong in wanting and seeking sovereignty. Many in the audience were relatively new to the sovereignty movement. They had mixed feelings about their presence there and about their participation in the movement. Deep down they knew their cause was just and what they were doing was right, but they also felt that they were doing something clandestine, something un-American. Some felt that what they were doing would not be approved of by the public, and that because of this, somehow their actions were wrong.

Wilkinson's message was that what was truly wrong was that they felt this way at all. If they only knew the facts, they would quickly see that theirs was the only just cause. Their nation had indeed been "illegally" overthrown. So much information had come to light in recent years that no historian any longer questioned that the United States conspired against the Hawaiian government and was responsible for its overthrow. Justice demanded that Hawaiians act. "Given what is known today, it is irresponsible and irrational for others to brand the movement for native sovereignty as 'radical.' The conspiracy and coup of 1893 which displaced the native sovereignty, **that** was radical."[31]

Wilkinson pointed out that Native Hawaiians have the strongest claim to sovereignty of any indigenous group in the United States because during the century before 1893, Hawai'i was recognized by the world as a sovereign nation. It had exchanged consuls and ministers with a number of governments. It had internationally recognized treaties with a number of powers. France and England **and the United States** had treaties with Hawai'i which guaranteed its independence as a sovereign nation. American Indians had no such claim to internationally recognized sovereignty; they were domestic groups. Yet look what sovereignty they have achieved.

The United States conspired to have your sovereign government toppled and your territory taken over by others. That is your grievance. Wilkinson said it was his view that

"Hawaiians are morally entitled to full international sovereignty, including membership in the United Nations."

Should Hawaiians want to pursue only the "nation within a nation" model, he noted that the Supreme Court has affirmed repeatedly that there are three sources of sovereignty in the United States: the federal government, state governments, and tribal governments. Hawaiians, along with the Alaskan Aleuts and Inuits and the American Indians in "the lower forty-eight," meet all of the federal requirements for treatment as native Americans. There is a dignified body of legal thought already worked out supporting the sovereignty of "native Americans." It is sitting there waiting to be applied in securing lands, self-government, and native rights as a nation within the United States.

Wilkinson urged Hawaiians to consider options beyond those taken by the American Indians, however. "Because **your claim is so clear, you can demand so much more. Hawaiian sovereignty should be sovereignty on Hawaiian terms.**"

Another point of interesting information discussed at the conference was that it was President Nixon who asked Congress to change its policy of terminating American Indian tribes. He and every president since have encouraged native Americans to maintain and to strengthen their independence.

Coincidentally, on the day following the conference, a special assistant to President Reagan was quoted in the newspapers as writing Chairman of the Office of Hawaiian Affairs, Moses Keale, that "President Reagan stands firmly behind his Indian Policy statement of 1983. That policy challenges the Indian people and Alaska natives to take responsibility for themselves and their communities, [it] reaffirms the government-to-government relationship, and the rights of tribes to determine the needs of their members and [to] establish and operate programs which best meet those needs."[32]

The Native Hawaiian Rights Conference ended on August 7, 1988, with a sense of unity. There was an unspoken consensus that there was value, at least temporarily, in the various groups remaining distinct. Having more groups would produce more diversified, better-thought-out ideas about the forms sovereignty might take.

There was also a consensus that they would speak unitedly of the need for sovereignty. Senator Inouye had called a Congressional hearing for August 21, 1988, to discuss future options the Hawaiians might pursue in their call for reparations. Plans were made to present the sovereignty issue at that hearing.

Senator Daniel K. Inouye

Few were prepared for the surprise at the Congressional hearing on August 21st, chaired by one of the U.S. Senators from Hawai'i, Daniel K. Inouye. After a number of representative groups of Hawaiians had given presentations for almost five hours, a number of them calling for nationhood rather than simply for money as reparations, the Senator spoke. He told how, a number of years before, he was selected as Chairman of the Senate Select Committee on Indian Affairs. No chairman before him had ever gone out to the reservations to see what was really happening, but he determined to go. He began visiting reservations and finding out what the people needed. In his travels he had become committed to the Indian people, to the preservation of their cultures, their rights as sovereign nations, and their needs. Over these years he had always been making comparisons between Indian and Hawaiian peoples. The reason he had called these hearings was not to waylay the movement for reparations for the overthrow of the monarchy, but rather to get it back on track in the Congress.

The senator acknowledged America's place in the overthrow of the Hawaiian government and welcomed the Hawaiian people to come to him with their program for restitution.

It was only a few years ago that one did not speak publicly of Hawaiian sovereignty, he said. It seemed treasonous. However, in recent years even people considered conservative in the community are talking about it. Some are now even discussing "autonomy."

Senator Inouye firmly announced that, "If native American Indians have sovereignty, it is difficult to argue that Hawaiians do not." "Hawaiian sovereignty is a legitimate issue that must be considered by the Select Committee on Indian Affairs and by the Congress."

The senator closed the meeting by asking the participants and other leaders of the Hawaiian community to meet with him on the following Wednesday.

At that meeting, he again stressed his support for Hawaiian sovereignty and self-determination. He told an anecdote of how he had run into a Hawaiian friend a day or so before, who had apologized to him for "all of this sovereignty talk" he was hearing. He told how he had to bring the man around to realize that he should be supporting the movement, that the time had come.[33]

Senator Inouye closed the meeting by pledging, "Within my lifetime, I will come to the inauguration of your first sovereign leader."[34]

The Hawaiians have been meeting. They have been educating their people, and providing forums for the people to discuss what they want in the way of autonomy. In December, 1988, under the leadership of Kekuni Blaisdell, the Center for Hawaiian Studies at the University of Hawai'i, the Native Hawaiian Legal Corporation, and six other groups sponsored a two-day Sovereignty Conference at the State Capitol in Honolulu. This brought together spokespersons from six of the major pro-sovereignty groups and provided them an opportunity to clearly state their stands on a number of issues.[35] The variety of ideas was impressive. They demonstrated clearly that it was not yet time to solidify on one stand. The Hawaiian people as a whole need to be presented a number of possibilities for future nationhood, and to have the time to explore them, so that when they are finally asked to vote, they will make the most enlightened choice. Since the conference, the various groups have continued to take their views out to the people.

A number of professors, doctors, lawyers, and long-time Hawaiian activists have formed The Pro-Hawaiian-Sovereignty Working Group. Their interest is to keep abreast of late happenings and to see through problems and smoke screens. Through their newsletter, *Ka Mana o Ka 'Aina*, they disseminate views on what is really happening behind the scenes, along with updated news of pro-sovereignty activities.[36]

On October 8, 1989, the Pro-Hawaiian-Sovereignty Working Group, in an effort to bring about a more united movement, invited leaders of the known pro-sovereignty organizations to a come together for a conference. They formed an organization called Ka Pākaukau (The Round Table).[37] As it has evolved, its membership has become completely native Hawaiian. It has lost a number of original member organizations over the years, but this has left it slim, trim, and fit. Through its spokesman, Dr. Kekuni Blaisdell, it quickly addresses developments and offers well-researched and documented Hawaiian responses.

Centennial Commemoration Edition Update

When *A Hawaiian Nation II   A Call for Hawaiian Sovereignty,* first appeared in February of 1990, the next chapter, "Possible Forms of Sovereignty," was reprinted on the front of the "Today" section of the combined Sunday *Star Bulletin & Advertiser.* The *Honolulu Advertiser,* then conducted a poll on what readers thought of Hawaiian sovereignty. Two-thirds of those answering supported Hawaiian nationhood. This strong support surprisingly came from people of all races.

Much has happened in the two years since. Numerous radio and television programs on sovereignty have aired, some scheduled regularly every week.

Churches and large civic organizations have spoken out in support. The state and the national governing bodies of both the United Church of Christ, one of the largest denominations in the islands, and of the Episcopal Church have taken formal positions of apology to the Hawaiian people for their inaction at the time of the Overthrow of the monarchy. Both, along with the American Friends (Quakers), have pledged themselves to actively support Hawaiian sovereignty.

In the political arena, the second-ranking member of the State House of Representatives, Vice Speaker Peter Apo, has produced an album of sovereignty songs. The album title, *A Call for Hawaiian Sovereignty--the Music*, ties the music to this book. Both Houses of the State Legislature and the governor of the state have given their implicit endorsement to the movement by forming and funding the Sovereignty Advisory Council, composed of eleven grass-roots organizations and state agencies, to do further study of models for Hawaiian nationhood. In 1991, the State legislature also voted for a resolution which would encourage debate on the restoration of the Hawaiian nation--"either within or without the United States." *(House Concurrent Resolution 147)* In 1992, the Legislature voted for a much stronger resolution, detailing the role of the United States in the Overthrow, stating that "the citizens of the State of Hawai'i recognize the inherent right of the indigenous Hawaiian people to sovereignty and self-determination," and calling upon the federal government to "assist in the establishment of a sovereign indigenous Hawaiian government, as requested by the Hawaiian people." *(Senate Concurrent Resolution 300)*

In national-level developments, in September 1991, a grant of nearly one million dollars was funded by an agency of the federal government, the Administration of Native Americans, to assist Hawaiians in educating their people and others about the issues of Hawaiian sovereignty and possible forms of future nationhood. The applicant for this grant was Hui Na'auao, an umbrella group composed of the many grass-roots pro-sovereignty organizations, the Office of Hawaiian Affairs, the Department of Hawaiian Homelands, Alu Like, the Hawaiian Civic Clubs, and many other Hawaiian organizations which had become interested in having a say about the development of the new nation. This education program is currently reaching out to Hawaiians statewide.

In Congress, Senator Daniel Inouye has drafted an initial version of a bill he wishes to introduce by which the United States in 1993 will recognize a body of elected Hawaiians as the Hawaiian nation, and begin negotiations with that nation.

The reason the Senator has been so willing to help on the reestablishment of the Hawaiian nation is because the Bush administration had stated its intent to do away with all of the special rights of the Hawaiian people on the grounds that, since there never was a treaty with the Hawaiian people, Hawaiians are no different from any other Americans in the melting pot and, according to the Constitution, cannot be treated any differently. In Inouye's view, only by Hawaiians asserting their sovereign nation status and winning American recognition for their nation can they protect their Hawaiian homestead lands, and all other rights and benefits they now have by law.

Following the Senator's request for comment on his bill, the Office of Hawaiian Affairs proposed three other sovereignty bills to establish the nation.

The summer of 1992 brought a round of activity for sovereignty. There were numerous demonstrations, marches, and other activities, and not just on Oʻahu: Kauaʻi, Molokaʻi, and the Big Island have all become quite active in sovereignty. The Democrats at their convention inserted a pro-sovereignty plank in their platform. A survey was published in the *Honolulu Star-Bulletin* that again demonstrated that the majority of the non-Hawaiians in Hawaiʻi feel that the Hawaiians should have some form of restitution for the loss of their nation. And the Kahoʻolawe Conveyance Commission moved towards its October 7th vote to return the island to Hawaiʻi.

Also happening on October 7, Senator Daniel Akaka got the U.S. Senate to approve a resolution which "apologizes to Native Hawaiians on behalf of...the United States for the illegal overthrow of the Kingdom of Hawaiʻi." It further commits Congress "to acknowledge the ramifications of the illegal overthrow" and to "provide a proper foundation for reconciliation." He expects to also get the resolution passed by the House of Representatives when they reconvene in January. And he is hopeful that the President will then sign on, and that the process of the restoration of the nation can begin in earnest.

As this book goes to print, a committee set up and funded by the legislature is planning a three-day commemoration of the overthrow of the monarchy on January 15, 16, and 17, 1993. A series of playlets will be broadcast both on radio and television which will reenact the actions that led to the overthrow during those three days a hundred years ago. Many sovereignty organizations are gearing up for activities to fill the days. Hopefully, there will be broad international news coverage, and the story of the Hawaiians and their desire for restoration of their nation will finally be widely told beyond our shores.

Possible Forms of Sovereignty

WHAT LANDS WOULD BECOME the sovereign Hawaiian nation? And what would the relationship of this nation be to the United States?

The form Hawaiian sovereignty will take should be decided by the whole Hawaiian people. Some models that have been proposed in recent years are discussed briefly here.

Nationhood Under the Aegis of the United States — "Nation within a Nation" The American Indian Model

There are 309 recognized nations within the territorial United States. American Indians, including Aleuts and Inuits, comprise the first 308. The 309th is the United States of America. Some of the sovereignty groups, such as the Office of Hawaiian Affairs and Ka Lāhui Hawai'i, and various individuals who have spoken or written publicly on the topic, are proposing nationhood within the territorial limits of the United States through a treaty or Congressional resolution with the United States. They want a sovereign status similar to that of the native American Indians.

Some people from these groups back this form of sovereignty because they think that America will never allow secession from the Union. The Civil War was fought to prevent secession, and even though the circumstances are entirely different, that war set the degree of commitment

131

and sacrifice Americans feel they must match in order to prevent secession. Others think that the American military would block secession, or that the one power even stronger than the military—financial interests—would prevent it. Some people support the "nation within a nation" concept because they see it as the first, more viable, step in a process of ultimate total separation. Others support it because they genuinely believe it is the most desirable form of sovereignty. Whatever their reasons, supporters are agreed that what is at least possible at the present time, is self-determination on somewhat the American Indian model.

Consider the "nation within a nation" model of an American Indian tribe: "Tribal" status entails sovereignty over members of a native group and control of an identified territory. Under this model, sovereignty is limited by the federal government, and the tribe must work with and within the American political and governmental system. But this type of sovereignty does include power to establish a preferred form of government, power to determine membership of the group, police power within native territory, power to administer justice with some limitations, power to exclude persons from native territory, and power to charter business organizations. Under this type of model, Hawaiians would not only have an identified land base, they would also have primary determination as to the development and management of the resources of their territory. The tribal model creates a solid basis for preserving cultural practices and values."[1]

Addressing the point of the land base which would become the "tribal territory," Hawaiians are asking for the return of the Ceded Lands. They would form the territory to be governed by the Hawaiian Nation and would provide the tax base to support that government. To give an example, much of downtown Honolulu is privately owned land; much of Kaneʻohe belongs to Castle Estate. Both would remain a part of the State of Hawaiʻi. But large sections of the Waiʻanae Coast are Ceded Lands, the "government lands" that were set aside by Kamehameha III for the benefit of his people. That area would become part of the Hawaiian nation, and follow the laws and pay taxes to the Hawaiian nation.

When the territory of the new nation is separated from the State, some Hawaiians speak of a willingness to make swaps of some Ceded Lands to arrive at greater contiguity. But they are not willing to wind up with only unproductive lands like they did with the Hawaiian Homes Act, nor are they willing to wind up with only country lands. They do not want to be land rich and money poor, another impoverished native people looked down on by American society because they cannot take care of themselves. Some of the highest tax generating entities in the State sit on Ceded Lands. The Hawaiian nation would need tax support, just as any nation does. Hawaiians should not be expected to trade the lucrative Honolulu International Airport for Kawainui Marsh.

If a form of the American Indian model is adopted, many Hawaiians seriously object to placing the Hawaiian nation under anything like a Bureau of Indian Affairs. History has shown that this would not be desirable. Many question whether any intermediary organization like the Bureau is necessary at all. They would have the United States deal directly with the Hawaiian nation, and have the nation do its own lobbying in Congress.

Those Indian tribes who have the greatest success in their relationships with the federal government deal with it on a "nation" to "nation" status. That is, they relate with it, not as *'ohana*s, or homestead organizations,[2] or island-of-Maui residents, nor as "tribes," nor as native American "peoples." Treaties have established the most successful tribes as **nations**. And they deal with the federal government "nation-to-nation," while remaining nations within a nation.

In a bold step, confident of nationhood, the Office of Hawaiian Affairs has begun a program to develop "tribal rolls," enrolling all people of Hawaiian ancestry. At present OHA intends to use this enrollment as a numerical power base to give it clout in negotiating with the federal government. State and national censuses show that there are more than 200,000 pure-blood and part-Hawaiian people living in Hawai'i, in continental America, and throughout the world. The enrollment will create a "tribal roll" of the members of the new Hawaiian nation, naming those who will come under its laws and share its benefits. Defining Hawaiian citizens through such a "tribal roll" is a necessary step if Hawaiians are to pursue "nation within a nation" status according to the American Indian model.[3]

A Distinctively Different, Broader Form of Hawaiian Sovereignty

Hawaiians have a totally unique situation. What they come up with in dealing with the federal government should be unique. This is not the early nineteenth century when most Indian treaties were signed; it is the end of the twentieth. Treaties with the American Indians can be used as precedents, but two hundred years of history offer valuable lessons about what is of value in treaties and what is not.

American Indian sovereignty is limited in various ways, and these limits have not served the Indians well. One area where Hawaiians may need broader rights involves international affairs. Hawaiians are part of the Polynesian race. Steps taken in the last two decades have reestablished and strenghthened those ties. Perhaps Hawaiians legitimately require the right to form pacts and treaties with the other peoples of the Pacific.

American Indian law-making and law-enforcement is limited. State laws apply on many Indian reservations. Given the number of Hawaiians who have difficulty with American laws, perhaps Hawaiians need their own system of law and justice, and complete freedom from state laws within Hawaiian territorial limits.

Taxation is limited among Indian tribes. Hawai'i is not an arid, desert area. It is a lush, productive island group, where taxation would make the difference between a prosperous nation and an impoverished one. Taxes collected on tourist dollars spent in the Hawaiian nation should stay in the Hawaiian nation.

If the "nation within a nation" concept is eventually adopted, it can be expected that it will include greater actual separation from the U.S. government and greater sovereignty than American Indians enjoy.

A plan being considered by Ka Lāhui Hawai'i would broaden Hawaiian independence by stages. Ka Lāhui

Hawai'i looks at the most sovereign of the Indian nations, the Iroquois, and sees that they have their own status at the United Nations separate from the United States. Iroquois also travel the world on their own passports. Their degree of sovereignty is indeed great. As a first step for the Hawaiian nation, Ka Lāhui proposes achieving—through treaty—recognition as a sovereign nation within the United States with "nation-to-nation" status like that of the Iroquois. This recognition would also include return of lands which would form the land base for the new Hawaiian nation.

Ka Lāhui Hawai'i would then move to place the Hawaiian land base on the United Nations' list of non-self-governing territories, since the land base still lies within the territory of the United States. This would place the Hawaiian nation under United Nations supervision and give it special guarantees of security accorded non-self-governing nations. It would also guarantee Hawaiians the right to further determine the kind of relationship they want with the United States. One relationship model being studied is "free association," such as is enjoyed by the Trust Territories of the Pacific. This would keep the Hawaiian nation within the American sphere of influence, but would allow it to interact freely in the international arena.[4]

Restoration of the Hawaiian Nation

Another model for sovereignty calls for total separation from the United States and restoration of the sovereign Hawaiian nation. Proposed by both Pōkā Laenui (Hayden Burgess) and by Peggie Ha'o Ross, and their followers, and supported now by many other groups, this call for a truly sovereign and independent Hawaiian nation simply recognizes that the overthrow of the Hawaiian monarchy was an illegal act of the United States government, and that the way for the United States to right that wrong is to withdraw from the islands and restore them to the rule of a Hawaiian nation. Supporters of this form of sovereignty contend that any settlement which in any way subordinates the Hawaiian islands to the United States is not a restoration of Hawaiian freedom and self-determination. They clearly are talking about total separation of Hawai'i from the United States.

One should not assume that the proponents of total Hawaiian sovereignty are madmen, or Communists, or traitors, or hot-headed revolutionaries. They are doctors and lawyers and professors and corporation executives, as well as small-business people and laborers and farmers and fishmen—who have studied their history, and who believe that the only just reparation for the overthrow of the Hawaiian nation is the return of native Hawaiian sovereignty in the form of an independent nation.

These individuals have gone to the World Council of Indigenous Peoples, to the United Nations, to the International Labor Organization, and to the World Court, to present the Hawaiian cause before these international bodies.

They point to a basic American tenet which Abraham Lincoln so well espoused in regard to Black slavery in the south: "No man has a right to rule over another without his consent." They accurately report that Hawaiians have never consented to rule by America. No native Hawaiian participated in the conspiracy that brought about the overthrow of the monarchy or in the overthrow itself. Hawaiians did not participate in the provisional government or in its decision to seek annexation. No vote of the people was taken to approve the treaty of annexation, or the establishment of the Territory of Hawai'i by the Congress. And when the votes for Statehood were taken, there were no statistics for how native Hawaiians voted, but the vote was phrased in such a way that the voter would remain an American citizen whatever the outcome. Hawaiians have never voted for union with the United States. Proponents of independence contend that Hawaiians would always have preferred their own nation.

Advocates of total separation foresee a restructuring of the new independent island nation around Hawaiian culture, Hawaiian expectations, and Hawaiian goals. They also recognize that they and the people who will constitute the citizenry are products of one hundred years of association with American ideals of democracy and principles of justice and fair play. These ideals and principles will continue to guide their actions. Proponents of total independence anticipate that basic American frameworks will have their place in guiding their formulations of government, just as will the structures adopted by the Hawaiian Kingdom in the past. They also recognize that private property and respect for its ownership were well established during the period of the monarchy.

Regarding citizenship, they note that citizens of the Hawaiian kingdom before 1893 included not only people with native Hawaiian blood, but also children born in Hawai'i, and people who went through the process of becoming naturalized citizens. Various groups active in the sovereignty movement hesitate to define points too precisely. By keeping concepts somewhat fluid or open to change, they keep the movement open to followers unable to support certain individual tenets. Statements on such things as what would constitute citizenship, therefore, are not nailed down. Pōkā Laenui feels that a real, living relationship with the land is basic, along with a devotion to Hawai'i and to native Hawaiian culture. He states, "The people I grew up with were from many races, but we all loved Hawai'i. We identified with the land. We knew we were Hawaiians." Citizens would at least be those with Hawaiian blood and others born here, if they pledged their support to the nation. "When it came to others...That's hard....I guess I would want to see attachment to the land, loyalty to the nation, and a real commitment to acculturation."

Some proponents also say that the independent nation should set its own policies on immigration. Recognizing that the present paving over of Hawai'i is taking place because of unbridled immigration, advocates of total separation would clamp an immediate freeze on immigration. A limit to the number of foreigners —non-citizens— who could live in the nation also would be set. Thinking ahead to what might happen with the establishment of an independent nation, proponents anticipate that some Americans may leave, wishing to live on American soil and under American laws. Envisioning a refocusing of the Hawaiian government away from fast growth and unchecked pursuit of the Yankee dollar, it is possible that other nationals would also move away. There could be a change in the balance of the races living in the new nation because of this.[5]

The nation many propose would truly be a Hawaiian nation, distinctively different in the world: a sovereign nation composed of people of many races who felt themselves a part of the islands and who sensed a oneness with the native people: a citizenry that supported the revitalization of Hawaiian culture with its traditional world view and approach to life. A Hawaiian nation ruled by Hawaiians. A nation not lost in its past, but embracing the present and the future from a uniquely Hawaiian perspective, and going about life in "the Hawaiian way."

Other Models for Sovereignty

Again, many variations are being developed from these basic models. Rather than demanding the whole archipelago for the new, totally independent Hawaiian nation, some speak of settling for parts of the islands, such as the Ceded Lands, or contiguous areas swapped for the Ceded Lands. Others speak of taking a number of islands for the independent Hawaiian nation, and letting the rest of the islands remain part of the United States.

How Nationhood Would Be Restored

A question not yet addressed is how sovereignty would be brought about. The answer varies with the type of sovereignty. If "native-American nation within the U.S. nation" status is decided upon, sovereignty would be granted by the Congress of the United States. Ordinarily this would be done by treaty, in which case the Senate alone would have to approve the treaty by a two-thirds majority. Seemingly, a native-American nation could also be established by a Resolution passed by a simple majority of both houses of Congress.

It can be an amazingly simple process. When the Menominee Indians were seeking the reestablishment of their tribe, one woman, Ada E. Deer, spent just one year in Washington lobbying legislators and lining up the votes of the Congress. When she was sure of enough votes to guarantee passage, the bill was moved to the floor, and the Menominees received not only the return of their tribal lands and tribal rights, but more than they began with when they signed papers of detribalization.[6] The Hawaiian situation is much more complex than that of the Menominees, but the process would be the same.

If the Hawaiian people decide they want a totally independent Hawaiian nation, they would also effect this by negotiating a treaty or a Resolution with the Congress of the United States. An international tribunal such as the United Nations would be asked to oversee the deliberations and to guarantee the decision.

What You Can Do

YOU CAN BECOME INVOLVED—become a real part of the process—even at the greatest distance. Most of the people in America are totally unaware that there is any problem. Talk about it. Get others interested and concerned for the Hawaiian people in their struggle for survival. Follow the progress of the sovereignty movement. But most importantly, write letters to the state legislators of Hawai'i and to national congresspersons.

Many Americans are caught up in the idea that America is always right, and that the way Americans think and act is best. But Americans have been wrong in Hawai'i. America has imposed its values and its economically-based lifestyle on the native people, and then to secure its hold, it has overthrown their monarch, toppled the government, and rewarded the agents of its actions with incredible wealth and power, while allowing them to reduce the native Hawaiian race to the lowest stratum of island existence. Since statehood, America has offered the islands to the rape of developers and speculators who have ignored the beautiful and scoffed at the sacred and pushed the cost of shelter so high that many native people are homeless.

There are few people on the face of the globe who so deeply commune with nature around them as do the Hawaiian people. The world-view which has given direction to Hawaiian life for two thousand years tells the Hawaiian that he is a participant in a conscious interrelating natural community from which he is descended and to which he is related as kin. This world-view gives him a sense of belonging, of "being at home in the world," a sense of fulfillment unknown to Western-thinking people.

For the Hawaiian, nature is alive. It cares for and protects him. And he must care for and protect it, as family. It is this world-view that causes him to stand defiantly in front of bulldozers. It is this world-view that is the driving force underlying his sovereignty movement. And it is this world view that eventually will save these islands, protect their beauty, and nurture their life. These lush islands are so precious, so fragile. So is the race that peoples them.

This is the Hawaiians' only homeland. There are no other Hawaiians "back home" preserving the race and the culture. There is no other "back home." When the Hawaiians' traditions have been completely lost and their blood dissipated until it causes no distinctive traits, the Hawaiians will be gone. For Hawaiians, the great and glorious American melting pot ideal is a black, boiling cauldron of extinction.

This is the time for action. The situation is urgent. More than a half million tourists a month are now visiting Hawai'i. And each month more tourists return to buy their cherished piece of the rock. Every lot or acre of virgin land sold for development further limits the possibilities for preserving undeveloped Hawaiian lands. With the rush to buy in Hawai'i, delay for even a few years may bring action too late.

Greater projects have come from nowhere and been accomplished within one or two years. Recent changes in Europe and the Soviet Union are examples.

Broad support is what is needed. Voice your concern. Write your Congressperson enlisting his or her assistance. Write and call your local news media, telling them you want more stories on what is happening in the Hawaiian sovereignty movement.

Help to bring forth that day when we all—Hawaiians and non-Hawaiians—can truly say, "*Ua mau ke ea o ka ʻāina i ka pono,* The life-breath of the lands continues now that things are set right again."

ENDNOTES

A History Of Dispossession

1 David E. Stannard, *Before the Horror: The Population of Hawai'i on the Eve of Western Contact*. Honolulu: Social Science Research Institute, University of Hawai'i, 1989. This book argues that the population of Hawai'i at the time of Cook's arrival in 1778 was 800,000 to one million. (Reviewed by Malcolm Naea Chun, "Book Review" *Ka Wai Ola O OHA, Iulai,* 1989, *'Ao'ao Ewalu.*) Stannard is not alone in arguing for the one million figure. A number of scholars in Hawaiian studies have been using that figure for some time.

2 Gavan Daws, *Shoal of Time: A History of the Hawaiian Islands,* Honolulu: University of Hawaii Press, 1974 (paper), p. 9.

3 Daws, *Shoal of Time,* p. 108.

4 Ralph S. Kuykendall, *The Hawaiian Kingdom,* Vol. I. Honolulu: University of Hawai'i Press, 1980, pp. 291-3. See also
Donald D. Kilolani Mitchell, *Resource Units in Hawaiian Culture,* Honolulu: The Kamehameha Schools Press, 1982, p. 262.

5 We are indebted to Lilikalā Dorton for the reasoning behind why the *mahele* was such a disaster: that native Hawaiians were **unable** to embrace it and make it work because 1)capitalism was diametrically opposed to all they had ever learned (The societal economy on the *ahupua'a* was based on generous giving. Capitalism is based on conserving, saving for one's self.) and 2)because the *ahupua'a* society satisfied all of their needs, natives did not know how to go about marketing their produce. She cites a passage in *The Works of the People of Old* (Samuel Kamakau, tr. by Mary Kawena Pukui, ed. by Dorothy Barrere, Honolulu: Bishop Museum Press, 1976, p. 122-3) where Kamakau tells that "peddling" was a practice despised by the ancestors. A peddler was held in extreme contempt.

Dorton's doctoral dissertation, *Land and the Promise of Capitalism: A Dilemma for the Hawaiian Chiefs of the 1848 Mahele,* is one of the first modern historical works written from the Hawaiian point of view. It was submitted to the History Department of the University of Hawai'i in December, 1986, and is available at Hamilton Library, University of Hawai'i. Since publishing this work, Dorton has reassumed the surname of her Hawaiian ancestors and is presently known as Lilikalā Kame'eleihiwa.

6 Daws, *Shoal of Time*, p. 125. See also Dorton, *Land and the Promise of Capitalism*, pp. 238-252.

7 Daws, *Shoal of Time*, p. 109. See also *Dorton, Land and the Promise of Capitalism*, pp. 238-52, for further amplification.

8 Armstrong Letters, Armstrong to Chapman, Sept. 18, 1844. Cited in Kuykendall, *The Hawaiian Kingdom*, I, p. 238.

9 Kuykendall, *The Hawaiian Kingdom*, I, p. 291. Also Daws, *Shoal of Time*, p. 125.

10 Wylie to Judd (No. 10) November 19, 1849, in *Report of Secretary of War*, 1855, Appendix   pp. 7-8.   Cited in Kuykendall, *The Hawaiian Kingdom*, I, p. 291.

11 Mitchell, *Resource Units in Hawaiian Culture*, pp. 263-4.   Also Kuykendall, *The Hawaiian Kingdom*, I, p. 294.

12 Act of 11 July 1851, [1851] Hawai'i Laws 52-3. We take this quote from Dorton, *Land and the Promise of Capitalism*, p. 316. She takes it from Neil M. Levy, "Native Hawaiian Land Rights," *California Law Review*, Vol. 63, no. 4 1975. p. 857. See also Kuykendall, *The Hawaiian Kingdom* I, p. 291 for variation. And see footnote 18 below.

13 Dorton, *Land and the Promise of Capitalism*, p. 316.

14 Dorton, *Land and the Promise of Capitalism*, p. 276.

15 We take this from Dorton, *Land and the Promise of Capitalism*, p. 316, who gives as a reference *Privy Council Records* II: 432-36.

16 Kuykendall, *The Hawaiian Kingdom*, I, p. 239.

17 Kuykendall, *The Hawaiian Kingdom*, I, p.297-8.

18 Co-author Dudley's translation. The source for this is *Kukini 'Aha'ilono*, ed. Rubellite Kinney Johnson, Honolulu: Topgallant, 1966, p. 52. which reads: *Oia na aina i haawiia mai e ko makou Alii Nui me ka maikai...ua hookaawaleia ua poe aina la no ke Aupuni Hawaii.... A ke koho aku nei makou i ke Kuhina Kalaiaina....E hiki i ke Kuhina Kalaiaina...ke hoolilo aku i na kanaka Hawaii na aina o ke Aupuni, ma kekahi ano e ae, a no na kumu e ae, ke maopopo ia ia a i mea pomaikai ai ke Aupuni.*

It might also be noted here that in the *Book of the Mahele*, as each of the divisions of land are listed, the paragraphs that head the crown lands, the chiefs' lands, and the government lands all state that the lands will belong to each of those three, but that the natives living on the land will have the right to claim their *kuleana*s from each of the new title holders. See pp. 52-4 in Johnson's *Kukini 'Aha'ilono* for the clause, *koe wale no ke kuleana o na kanaka e noho ana ma ua mau aina la*, "there remains only the *kuleana* of the people living on the aforesaid lands."

19   Act of 11 July 1851, [1851] Hawai'i Laws 52-3. We take this citing from Dorton, *Land and the Promise of Capitalism*, p. 316. She takes it from Neil M. Levy, "Native Hawaiian Land Rights," *California Law Review*, Vol. 63, no. 4 1975. p. 857. See also Kuykendall, *The Hawaiian Kingdom*, I, p. 291 for variation. And see footnote 16 above. See also *Native Hawaiians Study Commission*, Vol. I, p. 256.

20   Dorton, *Land and the Promise of Capitalism*, p. 265.

21   Kuykendall, *The Hawaiian Kingdom*, I, p. 336. See also the ftnt. on the same page. The native Hawaiian population was 103,790 in 1840; it was 99,626 in 1844; and 84,165 in 1850. The census of 1850 shows only 1,562 foreigners.

22   Kuykendall, *The Hawaiian Kingdom*, I, p. 230.

23   Kuykendall, *The Hawaiian Kingdom*, I, p. 240.

24   The *Buke Mahele* was signed on March 8, 1848. Dorton, *Land and the Promise*, p. 265.

25   Kuykendall, *The Hawaiian Kingdom*, I, p. 230.

26   Daws, *Shoal of Time*, p. 109.

27   Daws, *Shoal of Time*, p.109.

28   Dorton, *Land and the Promise of Capitalism*, p. 262   She is translating from the Privy Council Records IIIA:69. Dudley has altered the translation slightly, shifting words to make it read more clearly. Emphasis is Dorton's. Kuykendall also mentions, "The other and larger part, the king gave and set apart *forever* 'to the chiefs and the people.'" *The Hawaiian Kingdom*, I, p. 288.

29   Dorton, *Land and the Promise of Capitalism*, p. 264, quoting John Papa I'i, *Fragments of Hawaiian History*, 1959, p.50.

30   Dorton, *Land and the Promise of Capitalism*, p. 332. She cites the various *Privy Council Records* in her footnote to substantiate this claim.

31   Mitchell, *Resource Units in Hawaiian Culture*, p.263. See also Dorton, *Land and the Promise of Capitalism*, p. 265.

32   That this was the case is clear from a letter in *The Polynesian*, January 5, 1850, which is quoted in Kuykendall, *The Hawaiian Kingdom* I, p. 92.

33   Donald D. Kilolani Mitchell, *Resource Units in Hawaiian Culture*, p. 264. He is taking figures from *Hawaii Pono* by Lawrence H. Fuchs, New York: Harcourt, Brace and World 1961 p. 16.

34   *Native Hawaiian Study Commission*, Vol. I, p.257.

35 Dorton, *Land and the Promise of Capitalism*, p. 321. She cites Hobbs, Jean *Hawai'i: A Pageant of the Soil*, Stanford: Stanford University Press 1935, pp. 157-77.

36 Dorton, *Land and the Promise of Capitalism*, p. 321. She gives as a reference Amos Starr Cooke, *The Chiefs' Childrens School*, Honolulu: 1937, p. 349-50.

37 A. A. Smyser, "Annexation caused tears of joy—and sadness" *Honolulu Star-Bulletin*, Aug. 9, 1988. Editorial page.

38 Daws, *Shoal of Time*, p. 241 and passim.

39 It might be noted that the Hawaiian League at times also included native Hawaiians. A dissident faction under Robert Wilcox joined the *haoles*, seeking their own slate of reforms in government. It is clear, however, that these Hawaiians were not seeking Annexation and that they eventually split from the *haoles*. Robert Wilcox in fact led a rebellion to overthrow_ the bayonet constitution which the Hawaiian League imposed on Kalakaua.

40 Daws, *Shoal of Time*, p. 265.

41 Daws, *Shoal of Time*, p. 268.

42 Daws, *Shoal of Time*, p. 266-7.

43 Lili'uokalani *Hawaii's Story by Hawaii's Queen* Boston: Lee and Shepard 1898 p. 230-1.

44 Laenui, Pōkā (Hayden Burgess), *A Thief in Judgement of Itself*, Mms. available at 84-794-D Farrington Hwy., Wai'anae, HI 96792 p.8.

45 Daws, *Shoal of Time*, p. 272.

46 See President's *Message*—which comprises the following chapter in text.

47 Thurston, Lorrin A., *Memoirs of the Hawaiian Revolution*, Honolulu: Advertiser Publishing Co., 1936, pp. 230-2. I have taken this quotation from *The Native Hawaiians Study Commission*, Vol. I, p. 289.

Hawai'i Under Non-Hawaiian Rule

1 Kuykendall, Ralph S., *A History of Hawaii*, New York: Macmillan 1928, p. 280-1. Also, Daws, *Shoal of Time*, p. 279.

2 Daws, *Shoal of Time*, p. 281.

3 Daws, *Shoal of Time*, p. 281.

4 Daws, *Shoal of Time*, p. 285.

5 Cooke, Alistair, *America: A Personal History by Alistair Cooke*, a television series on the Public Broadcasting System. These notes are taken from the episode called, "Gone West." For additional support, see also footnote 6 below.

6 Calkins, Carroll C., ed. *The Story of America*, Pleasantville, N.Y.: Readers Digest, 1975, p. 71.

7 They were such people as: John Jay, who among many other things was a signer of Declaration of Independence, signed the Peace Treaty with England, was U.S. Secretary of State for Foreign Affairs, and also Governor of New York; John Langdon, delegate to the Continental Congress and Governor of New Hampshire; Elias Boudinot, elected to Congress, appointed by President Washington as Director of the Mint; John Treadwell, Governor of Connecticut; General Henry Sewell; and the businessmen, William Bartlett, William Phillips, and Robert Ralston. For more details see *Memorial Volume, American Board of Commissions for Foreign Missions, Half-Century*, Boston: Missionary House 1861, pp. 116-125. Available at Mission Houses Library, Honolulu.

8 Calkins, *The Story of America*, p. 82.

9 Sec. of Navy Robeson to Pennock, Dec. 25, 1872, Navy Dept., Letters to Flag Officers and Commandants of Vessels, No. [Vol.] 7. as quoted in Kuykendall, *The Hawaiian Kingdom*, II, p. 248. Insertion of "[Minister Pierce]" by Kuykendall.

10 Belknap to Schofield, confidential, June 24, 1872, War Dept. Records, quoted in Kuykendall, *The Hawaiian Kingdom*, II, p.248.

11 Schofield and Alexander to Belknap, May 8, 1873, printed in Sen. Ex. Docs., 52 Cong., 2 sess., no. 77, pp. 130-4. Quoted in Kuykendall, *The Hawaiian Kingdom*, II, p.248.

12 *Native Hawaiian Study Commission*, Vol. I, p. 267, which cites the Act of January 30, 1875, 19 Stat. 625-626.

13 *Native Hawaiian Study Commission*, Vol. I, p. 267, which cites Charles C. Tansill, *The Foreign Policy of Thomas F. Bayard*. New York: Fordham University Press, 1940, p. 370.

14 *Native Hawaiians Study Commission*, Vol. I, p. 274. They cite Bayard MS, Foreign Relations, 1894, Appendix II, pp. 660-662, 793-817, quoted in Tansill, *The Foreign Policy of Thomas Bayard*, p. 391-2.

15 Daws, *Shoal of Time*, p. 259.

16 Daws, *Shoal of Time*, p. 260-1.

17 Thurston, Lorrin A., *Memoirs of the Hawaiian Revolution*, Honolulu: Advertiser Publishing Co., 1936, pp. 230-2. I have taken this quotation from *The Native Hawaiians Study Commission*, Vol. I, p. 289.

18 Kuykendall, *The Hawaiian Kingdom* III, p. 567.

19 Kuykendall, *The Hawaiian Kingdom* III, p. 567.

20 Kuykendall, *The Hawaiian Kingdom* III, p. 567.

21 Kuykendall, *The Hawaiian Kingdom* III, p. 567-8.

22 Much of this information is also found in a manuscript for an article titled, "Cuba and Hawai'i," written by Carl Opio Young for the *Journal of the World Council of Indigenous Peoples*, Vol. 3. The authors are grateful to Sylvia Reck for bringing the article to their attention.

23 Kuykendall, *The Hawaiian Kingdom* III, p. 568.

24 Picture found in *Ka Mana O Ka 'Aina*, May/June 1969, p. 7.

25 Daws, *Shoal of Time*, p. 256-7.

26 Daws, *Shoal of Time*, p. 267-8.

27 Daws, *Shoal of Time*, p. 284.

28 Daws, *Shoal of Time*, p. 282.

29 See references to this in the 31st Congressional Record, p. 6702 (1898). Cited in *Native Hawaiian Study Commission* Vol I, p. 307.

30 Daws, *Shoal of Time*, p. 289-90.

31 Daws, *Shoal of Time*, p. 291.

32 Congress could change the Organic Act at will. Gavan Daws, *Shoal of Time*, p. 382.

33 Congress passed Public Law 88-233 on December 23, 1963 under which approximately 227,972 acres of national parks became the fee simple property of the federal government. (This information is found on p. 6 of a brochure with excerpts from a forth-coming *Native Hawaiian Rights Handbook* which was passed out by the Native Hawaiian Legal Corporation at the Native Hawaiian Rights Conference at Kamehameha Schools, August 5, 6, 7, of 1988.)
Linda Menton and Eileen Tamura, *A History of Hawai'i*, Honolulu: Curriculum Research and Development Group, Univeristy of Hawai'i, 1989, p. 317, give 143,700 acres of Ceded Lands as belonging to the military in Hawai'i.

34 *'Aina Ho'opulapula*, 1983-'84 Annual Report Department of Hawaiian Home Lands, p. 5.

35 *'Aina Ho'opulapula* 1983-'84 p. 7.

36 Fuchs, *Hawaii Pono*, p. 255.

37 Fuchs, *Hawaii Pono*, p. 173.

38 Fuchs, *Hawaii Pono*, pp. 252-3.

39 Fuchs, *Hawaii Pono*, p.253.

40 *Hawaiian Homes Commission Act*, Sixty-Seventh Congress. Session I, Chapter 42. 1921. Sec. 213.

41 Daws, *Shoal of Time*, p. 298.

42 Testimony given before Senator Daniel K. Inouye on August 21, 1988 by Ms. Julie Cachola. This figure was included in an earlier draft of this section which was reviewed by Kenneth Toguchi, news spokesperson for the Department of Hawaiian Home Lands. Asked for comments and corrections, he left this figure alone.

43 Figures copied from speeches at the Native Hawaiian Rights Conference, August 5-7, 1988, at Kamehameha Schools. Not challenged by Kenneth Toguchi of the DHHL during the discussion mentioned in footnote 42 above.

44 *Hawaiian Homes Commission Act*, Sec. 302.

45 Fuchs, *Hawaii Pono*, pp. 256-7.

46 Daws, *Shoal of Time*, p. 312-313.

47 Laenui, Poka (Hayden Burgess), *A Thief in Judgement of Itself*, mms., p. 22. We have edited this paragraph from the original.

48 Laenui, Poka (Hayden Burgess), *A Thief in Judgement of Itself*, mms., p. 22.

The Native Hawaiian Today

1 Much of this chapter is a rewriting of a guest editorial by Michael Kioni Dudley, "A Native Hawaiian Nation," published in *The Honolulu Star-Bulletin*, November 15, 1986.

2 Statistics for this chapter have been gathered from numerous places by co-author Dudley for the editorial mentioned in footnote 1. Many are also mentioned in the Action Alert, "OHA Moves to Break the Ceded Lands (5f) Trust," published by Ka Lahui in August, 1988. Many are also mentioned in the article "Native Hawaiian Illhealth: Hope for a Painful Paradox in 'Paradise,'" by Richard Kekuni Blaisdell, M.D., in the 1987 "Progress Edition" of the *Honolulu Star Bulletin*.

3 The Hawai'i State Department of Health "1986 Survey: Methods and Procedures, Heath Surveillance Survey" lists 8,244 Hawaiians with 100% Hawaiian blood.

The Need For A Hawaiian Nation

1 Samuel Manaiakalani Kamakau, "Ka Moolelo o Kamehameha I," in Ka Nupepa Ku'oko'a, August 24, 1867. Quoted in Ralph S. Kuykendall, The Hawaiian Kingdom, I, p.89.

2 Quote taken from The Ruling Chiefs, p. 204, a translation of Ka Nupepa Ku'oko'a, August 24, 1867. Archibald Campbell also states, "I have often seen the king working hard in a taro patch." A Voyage Around the World from 1806-1812, p. 116.

3 Sheldon Dibble, History of the Sandwich Islands, Honolulu: Thos. G. Thrum, 1909, p. 131.

4 Kuykendall, The Hawaiian Kingdom, I, pp. 72-3. Kuykendall has as his source the Letters of James Hunnewell dated July 15, 20, Aug. 2, 6, Sept. 21, 1820, which are found in the Harvard College Library.

5 William Ellis, Polynesian Researches Hawaii, Vol. IV. 1842. rpt. Rutland: Tuttle, 1969, p. 319.

6 Ellis, Polynesian Researches Hawaii, p. 319.

7 Kuykendall, The Hawaiian Kingdom I, p. 259. His source is unclear. In footnotes 130 and 132 on p. 258, he lists a number of sources for petititions he quotes. Most of these are found in AH FO & Ex. (Archives of Hawaii Foreign Office and Executive file.)

8 Kuykendall, The Hawaiian Kingdom I, p. 273 quoting from editorial in the Polynesian, October 25, 1845.

9 Letters of Dr. Gerritt P. Judd, pp. 180-182. Cited in Kuykendall, The Hawaiian Kingdom, I p. 279.

10 Quoted in 'Aina Ho'opulapula 1983-4 Annual Report, Department of Hawaiian Home Lands, p. 5.

11 A broader amplification of this entire discussion is found in the chapter "Confucianism," in Huston Smith, The Religions of Man. Harper Colophon Books Harper and Row: New York 1958, pp. 142-74.

12 The Hawai'i State Department of Health "1986 Survey: Methods and Procedures, Heath Surveillance Survey" lists 8,244 Hawaiians with 100% Hawaiian blood.

13 Helen B. Slaughter and Karen Watson-Gegeo, "Evaluation Report for the First Year of the Hawaiian Language Immersion Program," Department of Education, State of Hawai'i, June, 1988, p. 13.

14 "Complete results of Stanford Achievement Test scores in Hawaii public schools" *Honolulu Star-Bulletin*, Saturday, October 15, 1988, p. A-6.

The Sovereignty Movement—
Where it came from and where it is today

1 *Hawaiians: Organizing Our People*, a pamphlet produced by the students in "ES221—The Hawaiians" in the Ethnic Studies Program at the University of Hawai'i, Manoa, in May 1974, p.17. The pamphlet is available in the Hamilton Library at the University of Hawai'i, Manoa.

2 *Hawaiians: Organizing Our People*, p. 33.

3 *Hawaiians: Organizing Our People*, p. 37.

4 According to an advertisement in the *Ka Wai Ola O OHA*, March, 1989.

5 *Hawaiians: Organizing Our People*, p. 35.

6 McGregor-Alegado, Davianna, "*Hawaiians: Organizing in the 1970s*," *Amerasia* Vol. 7, No. 2 (1980) p. 45.

7 McGregor-Alegado, Davianna, "*Hawaiians: Organizing in the 1970s*." According to her footnote 46 on p. 55, the Congressional bills were "House Bill 1944, introduced 23 January 1975, to the 94th Congress; Senate Joint Resolution 155, introduced 18 December 1975; Senate Joint Resolution 4, reintroduced 10 January 1977; House Joint Resolution 526, introduced 21 June 1977.

8 Kamali'i, Kina'u Boyd, Chairperson, *Native Hawaiians Study Commission*, Vol. 2, p. x.

9 As he writes in the preface to his first work, *A History of Hawaii*:

The Legislature of the Territory of Hawaii, by laws enacted in 1921 and 1923 provided for the appointment of an Historical Commission. Among the duties assigned to this Commission was that of having compiled and published a school textbook of Hawaiian history. Governor Farrington appointed as members of the Commission, Hon. Jonah Kuhio Kalanianaole, Hawaii's Delegate to Congress [who died before the Commission began its activities], Hon. George Carter, formerly Governor of the Territory, and Dr. K.C. Lubrick, Professor of History in the University of Hawaii. Upon the death of Prince Kuhio in January, 1922, Mrs. A.P. Taylor was appointed to fill the vacancy. After its organization, the Commission employed Ralph S. Kuykendall as Executive Secretary. It is under the direction and by the authority of the Historical Commission as thus constituted that the volume (the "textbook of Hawaiian history" required by law) has been written. (Ralph S. Kuykendall, *A History of Hawaii*, New York: Mc Millan, 1926, see preface.)

10 Kuykendall perhaps wrote the preface quoted in the previous note as a disclaimer for what he knew was a biased view of Hawaiian history. But as time went on he gave up any efforts to see history from any but the American viewpoint. A short article on Hawaiian history, titled "Destined to be American," in a 1951 edition of the periodical, *American Heritage*, a period when he was totally free from the Commission and able to speak his mind, demonstrates his basic approach to Hawaiian history: Hawai'i was destined to be American. "Destined to Be American," *American Heritage*, Vol 2: No 3 (Spring 1951) pp. 31-3 and 76.

11 *Native Hawaiians Study Commission* Vol. I, p. 265.

12 *Native Hawaiians Study Commission* Vol. I, pp. 289-301 and endnotes.

13 Senator Daniel K. Inouye, "Opening Remarks," Hearing of the Select Committee on Indian Affairs, held in Honolulu, Hawai'i, August 28, 1988, concerning Native Hawaiian Reparations, p. 2.

14 Others joining Kamali'i were Winona K. D. Beamer, and H. Rodger Betts, both from Hawai'i.

15 McGregor-Alegado, Davianna, *"Hawaiians: Organizing in the 1970s,"* pp. 51-2. Though not an exact quotation, this is a close restatement of her material.

16 Other frequent spokesmen for 'Ohana O Hawai'i are Liko Martin and Steve Kamahana.

17 In a 1982 meeting of the Protect Kaho'olawe 'Ohana, "self determination for Native Hawaiians was officially adopted as a goal of the 'Ohana. In May 1987, we sought to clarify our position on sovereignty by stating that the 'Ohana supports the reestablishment of the Hawaiian nation and would participate in efforts to assert Hawaiian self-determination as a nation." Taken from the prepared statement of the representative from the Protect Kaho'olawe 'Ohana, Aloha "Maka" Makanani, to the Native Hawaiian Sovereignty Conference at the Hawai'i State Capitol, December 3-4, 1988.

The Protect Kaho'olawe 'Ohana has had so many active participants over the years that it would be impossible to give a listing of leaders without leaving out many names. In tribute to all the members, we will list the island reps named in a 1981 edition of their newspaper, *Aloha 'Aina*. Hilo: Moanikeala Akaka, Kona: Earl DeLeon, Kohala: Clyde Dement, Ka'u: Palikapu Dedman, Maui: Malia Bisquera, Hana: Uncle Harry Mitchell, Lana'i: Sol Kaho'ohalahala, Moloka'i: Judy Napolean, Kaua'i: Donna A'ana, O'ahu: Bo Kahui, Georgette Meyers. Today some leaders of the group include Davianna McGregor-Alegado, Aloha "Maka" Makanani, and Keoni Fairbanks.

18 Two spokespersons for the Save Nukolii Committee are John Pilkington and Jo Soares, according to an article, by John Witeck, "Nukolii: Round Two" *Ka Huliau*, October-November 1983, pp. 4-5.

19 Spokespersons for the Hui Alanui o Makena are Dana Naone Hall and Isaac Hall.

20 Some of the leaders in the Save West Beach protests were Eric Enos, Ho'oipo De Cambra, Puanani Burgess, Hayden Burgess, Walter Kealiiokekai Paulo, Ray Catania, John Kelly, Mike Kahikina.

21 Bernard Punikaia and Clarence Naia were arrested along with sixteen supporters in a dawn raid on this hospital. Then the buildings were destroyed. John Witeck, "Dawn raid at Hale Mohalu," *Ka Huliau* October-November, 1983, p. 1.

22 Dr. Emmett Aluli and Palikapu Dedman are leaders of this fight. They have formed the Pele Defense Fund and are challenging court decisions against them. The Office of Hawaiian Affairs, at this writing, is considering a stand in their support.

23 Ka 'Ohana O Kalae was formed in 1982 to oppose the proposed use of Hawaiian Homes land for commercial satellite launches. It also opposes expansion of the small boat harbor there. Spokespersons for the group include Keola Hanoa and Palikapu Dedman. (Rod Thompson, "Activist Group Wants Priority for Hawaiians on South Point Land" *Honolulu Star Bulletin*, July 28, 1986, p. A-3).

24 This movement won widespread support from people all over the state. It would be impossible to name all of even the prominent activist leaders who became actively involved. As an attempt to put at least some names on record, Ed and Puanani Kanahele, Davianna McGregor-Alegado, Palikapu Dedman, Dana Hall, Marion Kelly, and Soli Niheu are some of the names that have come to the authors.

25 This information was given to Dudley in a conversation with Mililani Trask.

26 Other members of this organization include Puhipau Ahmad, Kalama and Puanani Akamine, Peter Kealoha, Kealiiokekai Paulo, Leianuenue Niheu, Leina'ala Kaina, Joan Beuhring and Kekuni Blaisdell.

27 Testimony given by the Office of Hawaiian Affairs at the Hearing of the Select Committee on Indian Affairs, held in Honolulu, Hawai'i, August 28, 1988, concerning Native Hawaiian Reparations. Other current trustees of OHA are Thomas Kaulukukui, Louis Ha'o, Manu Kahaialii, Moses Keale, and Kevin (Chubby) Mahoe.

28 *Ka Wai Ola O OHA, Malaki,* 1989, *'Ao'ao iwakaluakumakahi.*

29 This section is a compilation of material taken from co-author Dudley's notes and from an article, "Native Hawaiian Rights Conference

Theme is Hawaiian Sovereignty—"The Ultimate Unity"? by Deborah Lee Ward. Her article is found in *Ka Wai Ola O OHA Kepakemapa*, 1988 *'ao'ao umikumalua-umikumakolu.* Many of these thoughts are taken from the talk by John E. Echohawk, a member of the Pawnee Tribe, a lawyer, and the executive director of the Native American Rights Fund.

30   *Ka Wai Ola O OHA Kapakemapa*, 1988 *'ao'ao umikumaha.*

31   These quotations are taken from the article in *Ka Wai Ola O OHA* (*Kapakemapa*, 1988 *'ao'ao umikumaha*) and from notes of co-author, Dudley, taken at the conference.

32   "White House defends Indian remarks," *Honolulu Star-Bulletin*, Monday, August 8, 1988 p. A-5.

33   These comments are taken from the notes of the co-author, Dudley, taken at the conference.

34   These comments are taken from the notes of the co-author, Dudley, taken at the conference.

35   Position papers were presented by Louis "Buzzy" Agard (Council of Hawaiian Organizations), Imaikalani Kalahele (Na 'Oiwi O Hawai'i), Mililani Trask (Ka Lahui Hawai'i), 'Iwalani Minton (E Ola Mau), Alohawaina Makanani (Protect Kaho'olawe 'Ohana), and presenting for Poka Laenui, his daughter Pua'ena Burgess (Institiute for the Advancement of Hawaiian Affairs). Moderators for the conference were Dr. Naleen Andrade and Keoni Agard. John Dominis Holt and Haunani Kay Trask gave the keynote addresses.

36   Among those who regularly attend Pro-Hawaiian-Sovereignty Working Group meetings are Kekuni Blaisdell, Louis "Buzzy" Agard, Stephen Boggs, Marion Kelly, Tom Maunupau, Sylvia Keewson Reck, Mililani Trask, Maivan Lam and Kioni Dudley. Copies of *Ka Mana O Ka 'Aina* are available from P.O. Box 27-478 Honolulu, Hawai'i 96827

37   Members of the Steering Committee of Pakaukau are Richard Kekuni Blaisdell (Interim Chairman), Melia Melemai (Secretary), Peggie Ha'o Ross, Mililani Trask, Soli Niheu, Louis Buzzy Agard, Kawehi Gill, Sam and Virginia Kepano, Frank Nobriga, Aloha Maka Makanani, Davianna McGregor-Alegado, Kamuela Kealoha, and Sonny Kaniho.

Possible Forms Of Sovereignty

1   This paragraph, with slight changes, was taken from a forty-page untitled manuscript, and seems to be excerpted from the *Native Hawaiian Rights Handbook* which is scheduled for publication in mid-1989.

2   The State Council of Hawaiian Homestead Associations, headed by Kamaki Kanahele, in a July, 1989, meeting decided to seek

self-governance on the lands set aside for them by Congress. Reports of this meeting indicate that the Homestead Associations are not interested in "sovereignty." They do, however, want to gain control of the Hawaiian Home Lands and "other assets that are trusts of the Hawaiian people." (Stu Glauberman, "Third Hawaiian group enters self-determination fight," *Honolulu Star Bulletin*, July 25, 1989.) Critics see this as settling for too little. But more importantly they see it as choosing to deal with the federal government from a self-determination model that has not been effective for other Native American groups—a council of homestead associations. They point out that Hawaiians will have the most successful relationship with the federal government in the future if they organize themselves as a sovereign **nation** within the American nation and deal with the federal government "nation" to "nation."

3 The "Blueprint for Native Hawaiian Entitlements" is available at the Office of Hawaiian Affairs, Honolulu, Hawai'i.

4 This material is based on conversations between co-author Dudley and Mililani Trask, *kia'aina of Ka Lahui Hawai'i.*

5 Much of the material in this section is based on conversations between co-author Dudley and Poka Laenui (Hayden Burgess).

6 From the notes taken by co-author Dudley during the Conference on Native Hawaiian Rights, August 5-7, 1988, at The Kamehameha Schools.

BIBLIOGRAPHY

Aloha 'Aina. Newspaper of the Protect Kaho'olawe 'Ohana. Winter, 1981. Published by the Protect Kaho'olawe Fund, P.O. Box H, Kaunakakai, Moloka'i, Hawai'i 96748.

Blaisdell, Richard Kekuni M.D. "Native Hawaiian Illhealth: Hope for a Painful Paradox in 'Paradise,'" *Honolulu Star-Bulletin* "Progress Edition," 1987.

"Blueprint for Native Hawaiian Entitlements" Office of Hawaiian Affairs, September 2, 1989.

Calkins, Carroll C., ed. *The Story of America*. Pleasantville, N.Y.: The Reader's Digest, 1975.

Campbell, Archibald. *A Voyage Round the World From 1806 To 1812*. 1820 rpt. Honolulu: University of Hawaii Press, 1967.

Ching, Clarence F.T. "On Sovereignty," *Ka Wai Ola O OHA*. Vol. 6, No. 3. *Malaki*, 1989 *'Ao'ao* 21.

Chun, Malcolm Naea. "Book Review," *Ka Wai Ola O OHA, Iulai,* 1989, *'Ao'ao Ewalu*.

"Complete results of Stanford Achievement Test scores in Hawaii public schools" *Honolulu Star-Bulletin*, Saturday, October 15, 1988, p. A-6.

Cooke, Alistair. "Gone West," an episode in the series, *America: A Personal History by Alistair Cooke*. Shown on the Public Broadcasting System in 1989.

Cooke, Amos Starr. *The Chiefs' Childrens School*. Honolulu 1937.

Daws, Gavan. *Shoal of Time*. Honolulu, University of Hawaii Press, 1974.

Dibble, Sheldon. *History of the Sandwich Islands*. Honolulu: Thos. G. Thrum, 1909.

Dorton, Lil'kala (Kame'eleihiwa, Lilikala). *Land and the Promise of Capitalism: A Dilemma for the Hawaiian Chiefs of the 1848 Mahele*. A Dissertation. December, 1986. Available at Hamilton Library, University of Hawai'i at Manoa.

Dudley, Michael Kioni. "A Native Hawaiian Nation." *The Honolulu Star-Bulletin,* a guest editorial, November 15, 1986.

————. *The Bite of Food That Destroyed a Civilization, 'Ai Noa.* a study module for junior and senior students in high school. Honolulu: Hawaiian Studies Office, Department of Education, State of Hawai'i, 1987

————. *A Philosophical Analysis of Pre-European-Contact Hawaiian Thought* A Doctoral Dissertation. Available at Hamilton Library, University of Hawai'i.

Ellis, William. *Polynesian Researches: Hawaii*. Vol. IV. 1842. rpt. Rutland: Tuttle, 1969.

"From the Congressional Record 'Tributes to Prince Kuhio,'" *Ka Nuhou News* from the Department of Hawaiian Home Lands. Vol. 14, No. 1, March-April 1988.

Fuchs, Lawrence H. *Hawaii Pono.* New York: Harcourt, Brace, and World, 1961.

Glauberman, Stu. "Third Hawaiian group enters self-determination fight," *Honolulu Star Bulletin*, July 25, 1989.

Hawaiian Homes Commission Act. Sixty-Seventh Congress. Session 1, Chapter 42, 1921.

"Hawaiian Homes Commission Act, 1920," *'Aina Ho'opulapula* 1983-84 Annual Report of the Department of Hawaiian Home Lands. pp. 4-7.

Hawaiians: Organizing Our People a pamphlet produced by the students in "ES221—The Hawaiians" in the Ethnic Studies Program at the University of Hawai'i, Manoa, in May 1974. The pamphlet is available in the Hamilton Library at the University of Hawai'i, Manoa. Davianna McGregor-Alegado and Terrilee Kekoolani were co-project leaders.

Hobbs, Jean. *Hawai'i: A Pageant of the Soil.* Stanford: Stanford University Press, 1935.

Holt, John Dominis. *On Being Hawaiian.* Honolulu: Topgallant, 1964.

———. *Hawaiian Monarchy.* Honolulu: Hogarth Press, 1971.

———. *Kaulana Na Pua.* Honolulu: Topgallant, 1974.

Ii, John Papa. *Fragments of Hawaiian History.* From articles in *Ka Nupepa Kuokoa*, 1866-70. Translated by Mary Kawena Pukui. Honolulu: Bishop Museum Press, 1959.

Inouye, Senator Daniel K. "Opening Remarks," Hearing of the Select Committee on Indian Affairs, held in Honolulu, Hawai'i, August 28, 1988, concerning Native Hawaiian Reparations, p. 2.

Jarves, James J. *History of the Hawaiian or Sandwich Islands.* Boston: Tappan and Bennet, 1843.

Johnson, Rubellite Kinney, ed. *Kukini 'Aha'ilono.* Honolulu: Topgallant Press, 1966.

Kamakau, Samuel Manaiakalani. *Ruling Chiefs of Hawaii.* Honolulu: The Kamehameha Schools Press, 1961.

———. "Ka Moolelo o Kamehameha I," *Ka Nupepa Ku'oko'a.* August 24, 1867.

———. *The Works of the People of Old.* Tr. by Mary Kawena Pukui. Ed. by Dorothy Barrere. Honolulu: Bishop Museum Press, 1976.

Kamali'i, Kina'u Boyd, Chairperson. *Native Hawaiians Study Commission*, Vol. 1. June 23, 1983.

———. Native Hawaiians Study Commission, Vol. 2, June 23, 1983.

Ka Mana O Ka 'Aina. Bulletin of the Pro-Hawaiian Sovereignty Working Group. P.O. Box 27-478 Honolulu, Hawai'i 96827

Kame'eleihiwa, Lilikalā (Lilikalā Dorton). *Land and the Promise of Capitalism: A Dilemma for the Hawaiian Chiefs of the 1848 Mahele. A Dissertation.* December, 1986. Available at Hamilton Library, University of Hawai'i at Manoa.

Kamehameha III. (Kauikeaouli). Address to the People at the time of Cession of Hawaii to Lord George Paulet. Found in "Foreign Office and Executive Broadside" for February 11, 1843. This may be located at the State Archives, Honolulu, Hawaii.

Kuykendall, Ralph S. *A History of Hawaii,* New York: Mc Millan, 1926.

———. *The Hawaiian Kingdom.* Three Volumes. Honolulu: The University Press, 1938 - 1957.

———. "Destined to Be American," *American Heritage,* Vol 2: No 3, (Spring 1951) pp. 31-3 and 76.

Laenui, Poka (Hayden Burgess). "A Thief in Judgement of Itself." Mms. dated July 10, 1983. Write 86-630 Puuhulu Rd., Wai'anae, Hawai'i 96792.

Levin, Stephenie Seto. "The Overthrow of the *Kapu* System in Hawaii." *Journal of the Polynesian Society,* LXXVII (October, 1968), 408-28.

Levy, Neil M. "Native Hawaiian Land Rights," *California Law Review.* Vol. 63. No. 4. 1975.

Lili'uokalani, Queen. *Hawaii's Story by Hawaii's Queen.* Boston: Lee and Shepard. 1898.

Mc Gregor-Alegado, Davianna. *Hawaiian Resistance 1887-9.* A Thesis. Available at Hamilton Library, University of Hawai'i at Manoa.

———. "Hawaiians: Organizing in the 1970s." *Amerasia Journal,* Vol. 7, No. 2. (1980) pp. 29-55.

———. *Hawaiians: Organizing Our People* a pamphlet produced by the students in "ES221—The Hawaiians" in the Ethnic Studies Program at the University of Hawai'i, Manoa, in May 1974. The pamphlet is available in the Hamilton Library at the University of Hawai'i, Manoa. McGregor-Alegado was co-project leader with Terrilee Kekoolani.

Menton, Linda and Tamura, Eileen. *A History of Hawai'i.* Honolulu: Curriculum Research and Development Group, University of Hawai'i, 1989.

Memorial Volume, American Board of Commissions for Foreign Missions, Half-Century. Boston: Missionary House 1861.

Mitchell, Donald D. Kilolani. *Resource Units in Hawaiian Culture.* Honolulu: Kamehameha Schools Press, 1982.

Native Hawaiian Rights Handbook Mms. quoted here. Subsequently published by Native Hawaiian Legal Corporation, 1989.

Native Hawaiians Study Commission. Vol. 1. Kina'u Boyd Kamali'i, Chairperson. June 23, 1983.

Pogue, John F. *Moolelo of Ancient Hawaii.* 1858. Translated by Charles W. Kenn. Honolulu: Topgallant, 1978.

Slaughter, Helen B. and Watson-Gegeo, Karen. "Evaluation Report for the First Year of the Hawaiian Language Immersion Program," Department of Education, State of Hawai'i, June, 1988.

Smyser, A. A. "Annexation caused tears of joy—and sadness," *Honolulu Star-Bulletin.* Aug. 9, 1988. Editorial page.

Stannard, David E. *Before the Horror: The Population of Hawai'i on the Eve of Western Contact.* Honolulu: Social Science Research Institute, University of Hawai'i, 1989.

Sterling, Elspeth P. and Summers, Catherine C. *Sites of Oahu.* Honolulu: Bishop Museum Press, 1978.

Tamura, Eileen, and Menton, Linda. *A History of Hawai'i.* Honolulu: Curriculum Research and Development Group, University of Hawai'i, 1989.

Tansill, Charles C. *The Foreign Policy of Thomas F. Bayard.* New York: Fordham University, 1940.

Tate, Merze. *Hawaii: Reciprocity or Annexation.* East Lansing: Michigan State University Press, 1968.

Thompson, Rod. "Activist Group Wants Priority for Hawaiians on South Point Land," *Honolulu Star-Bulletin.* July 28, 1986. P. A-3.

Thurston, Lorrin A. *Memoirs of the Hawaiian Revolution.* Honolulu: Advertiser Publishing, 1936.

Turner, George. *Nineteen Years In Polynesia,* London, 1861.

Uprichard, Brett. "Dr. Emmett Aluli," *Honolulu* Magazine. July, 1988.

Ward, Deborah Lee. "Native Hawaiian Rights Conference Theme is Hawaiian Sovereignty—"The Ultimate Unity"? *Ka Wai Ola O OHA Kepakemapa,* 1988 *'ao'ao umikumalua-umikumakolu.*

Watson-Gegeo, Karen and Slaughter, Helen B. "Evaluation Report for the First Year of the Hawaiian Language Immersion Program," Department of Education, State of Hawai'i, June, 1988.

"White House defends Indian Remarks," *Honolulu Star-Bulletin.* August 8, 1988. P. A-5.

Witeck, John. "Nukolii: Round Two," *Ka Huliau.* (P.O. Box 61337 Honolulu, Hi 96822) October-November 1983, pp. 4-5.

———. "Dawn raid at Hale Mohalu," *Ka Huliau.* October-November 1983, p. 1.

Young, Carl Opio. "Cuba and Hawai'i," mms. prepared for *Journal of the World Council of Indigenous Peoples,* Vol. 3.

INDEX

Index of the Message to Congress by President Grover Cleveland

Order Form

A Hawaiian Nation I   Man, Gods, and Nature
by Michael Kioni Dudley
          Hard cover $19.95 _____
          Paperback $12.95 _____

A Call for Hawaiian Sovereignty
by Michael Kioni Dudley and Keoni Kealoha Agard
          Hard cover $19.95 _____
          Paperback $12.95 _____

A Green Hawai'i Sourcebook for Development Alternatives
by Ira Rohter
          Hard cover $25.95 _____
          Paperback $16.95 _____

                 Subtotal $ _____
      Postage and Handling $ __1.50__
              Total due $ _____

Name_____

Address_____

City_____State_____Zip_____

Send order to:
          Na Kane O Ka Malo Press
            P.O. Box 970
        Waipahu, Hawai'i 96797-0970
       Phone (808) 672-8888 or 677-9513